Designing and Making Fine Furniture

by John Chaffee

A & W Visual Library
New York

I would like to give special thanks to Donald Biggioni, A.I.A., for the design of the unit appearing on the front cover, and to Guenter Lange for the design of the coffee table in Project 16. I am also grateful to Steven LaRocca, A.I.A., for his assistance in the preparation of the diagrams.

Published by
A & W Publishers, Inc.
95 Madison Avenue
New York, New York 10016

ISBN 0-89104-095-1 (paperback)
ISBN 0-89104-096-X (hardcover)
Library of Congress Catalog Card Number: 78-53410
Designed by Fran Miskin
Printed in the United States of America

Designing and Making
Fine Furniture

For Heide, who made this book possible.
And for my parents, who made me possible.

Contents

Introduction

In an age of synthetics and mass production, quality wood furniture holds the same sort of attraction it has held for centuries. Perhaps this attraction is due to the fact that this wood was once a living organism, that its texture, grain, and coloring are part of nature's handicraft, unlike most of the artifacts we are surrounded with today. Perhaps it is due to its durability and resiliency, enabling it to survive generations, gaining in beauty as it ages. Whatever the explanation for wood's attractiveness, the fact is that good wood furniture is difficult to come by today. With the extensive modern-day use of plywood, fiberboard, veneers, and plastic laminates, the wood that you think you see is seldom the wood that you get.

In addition, the selection and purchase of wood furniture is often a hit-or-miss proposition, like buying clothes off the rack instead of having them custom tailored. It is a very challenging task indeed to find a piece of furniture that is the appropriate size, design, and color for your apartment or house, at a price that will not put you on the street selling pencils.

The purpose of this book is to enable you to aesthetically enhance and functionally maximize your living space by constructing quality wood furniture specifically tailored to your needs, your living environment, and your personal taste as well as your budget.

It's been my experience that most traditional and current books on the subject of furniture construction fall into one of two categories: Either they are very elementary descriptions of the use of woodworking tools coupled with very simple, commonplace furniture projects, or else they are extremely technical accounts with advanced and complex furniture projects, beyond the interest and capabilities of most people. In addition, both types characteristically limit themselves to the design of the actual piece of furniture and are not concerned with the overall environment in which the furniture will be placed.

This book attempts to be different by enabling you to construct imaginative, functional, and fine-quality furniture utilizing relatively simple techniques, in the same way that simple building blocks may be used to build complex structures. And instead of contemplating these pieces of furniture in splendid isolation, this book includes an examination of the basic design problems that any living space must deal with and demonstrates how the furniture designs must relate to the design of the living space as a whole as well as how these furniture designs can be combined and interrelated. It also emphasizes the utilization of living space to the fullest extent possible, particularly when this space is limited.

The heart of this book is a series of original furniture designs, illustrated with drawings and photographs, which I have designed and built. It includes designs for types of furniture that have recently evolved and become popular (loft beds, platform beds, wall units, room dividers) as well as unique and contemporary designs for traditional furniture (bookcases, tables, desks). These designs include modular furniture (where the individual parts of a whole can be rearranged in different combinations), built-in furniture (where the furniture is custom-built into the individual requirements of a specific space), and traditional freestanding furniture. All of these are designed so that they can be easily disassembled, moved, and reassembled. Above all, the designs are for fine-quality furniture that is built to withstand the vicissitudes of time. They form a solid nucleus of plans that can be adapted to fit the design and decor of virtually any living space.

Conceptually speaking, this book aims at encouraging you to see your living space as an extension of yourself, decorated and furnished in a manner that expresses your individual needs and tastes. The epitome of putting the stamp of individuality on one's living space is to utilize furniture constructed on a custom basis. This is also the only way to insure the maximum use of a limited space. Unfortunately, the cost of custom design and construction by someone else is often prohibitively high.

This book is designed to enable you to construct this sort of custom furniture yourself, allowing you to save anywhere from a significant amount of money to a small fortune. And, of course, it gives you the means to experience something beyond price—the satisfaction and pride of enjoying a personal relation with a custom piece of furniture that you have fashioned and crafted to your own specifications.

—John Chaffee
New York

Part One
The Fundamentals

Principles of Design

The act of building a piece of furniture for your living space can be thought of as a process stretching from the initial conception to the final actualized piece. The initial conception normally consists of a whole constellation of aesthetic ideas and functional needs that you bring with you into a situation. Many of these ideas are competitive, mutually incompatible, and even contradictory, and it takes time and thought to sort them out and mold them into a unified whole. There are a number of considerations and concepts that I have found useful in expediting this process. I believe that you will find an examination of them helpful in developing designs for furniture in your own living space.

Function

Chief among your considerations in arriving at a design is the purpose that the piece is going to serve. There has always been the chicken-and-the-egg controversy regarding the concepts of function and design—i.e., which of the two has preeminence over the other. I believe that for the purpose of constructing custom furniture, function should be the primary consideration and design should be developed once the function has been established. To those purists who would disagree with this view, I would say that there are a virtually infinite variety of potential designs, but if a piece does not fulfill the purpose for which it was originally intended, then it has failed as an object for human use.

When initially considering the function of your proposed project, you should not be reluctant to itemize the specific requirements it will be expected to fulfill. For example, in the case of a wall unit, questions like the following must be answered: How many books are to be accommodated? What heights are they? Are there objets d'art or things near and dear to you that you want accented or highlighted? At what heights do you watch TV and change records? And so on.

Taking an inventory like this might not be the most exciting way to initiate your project, but it is eminently practical, and it gives you a firm matrix upon which to weave your more creative and individual ideas.

Consider the wall unit in figure 129 (page 165). The person for whom it was built first made an exhaustive list of the things that were to be contained in the unit. When this was done, a design was developed that was both practical and pleasing to the eye, exhibiting an overall symmetry and balance. Spaces were created to highlight specific items and to break up the monotony of book-lined shelves. Finally, the unit was integrated into the rest of the room and its furnishings, plants, rugs, etc., creating a mosaic of form, texture, and color that challenges the perception without losing its appearance as a unified, structural whole.

Certainly in this case, design did not suffer at the hands of function.

Activity Patterns

Another factor to consider in designing furniture for yourself and arranging it in the space where you live or work is the concept of activity patterns. Your movements and activities in your living space are not random and chaotic. Instead, if a statistical study were to be performed, it would no doubt indicate certain recognizable patterns that characterize the way you live in that space. For example, although there may be a great variety of ways in which you *might* walk and move around your home, the truth is that most of us choose a limited number of ways or paths in which we comport ourselves. As a matter of fact, if two people have similar patterns in the same space, they may find themselves getting in each other's way, even though there may be plenty of room around them.

The same principle applies to the time we spend in other activities, such as reading, watching TV, studying, relaxing. Most people select certain favorite spots in which they spend their time, even though they could, theoretically at least, spend it in other positions.

These patterns of activity are in part dictated by the placement of the furniture, windows, doors, etc., and in part by your own idiosyncratic preferences. However, the origins of these patterns don't really matter; what is important is that you recognize them and integrate into them whatever new furniture designs you are contemplating. It you don't, you may find that you have arranged your furnishings in a way that may be aesthetically pleasing but that clashes with your natural patterns of activity.

Discovering these activity patterns and utilizing this information in the design of your living space, instead of merely relying on abstract aesthetic principles or what has a pleasant appearance, is a procedure founded upon the same bias for the functional and useful that we just considered. In order to feel comfortable in the spaces you inhabit, the *human* dimensions of your living experience must be considered prior to the purely formal, aesthetic, and factual dimensions. For the truth of the matter is this: If you can't expect to feel comfortable in your own home, then you're facing the rest of the world at a real disadvantage.

Measurement

Another aspect of environmental construction that has a human dimension as well as a factual, objective one is that of measurement. While the accuracy of measurements in objective terms (inches, centimeters, etc.) is an absolutely essential aspect of successful furniture construction (about which I will go into detail in the next chapter), the idea of *human* measurement is just as essential and actually takes logical precedence over the other.

For example, imagine you are attempting to determine the measurements for a coffee table you want to build. The initial questions to ask are ones like: What height is comfortable when you are seated in front of it? What width will still allow access to the couch? Will you be able to cross your legs in front of it? Is it a size that allows you to move it to another spot in the room yet still fit it into the overall design of that room?

These are questions whose answers are ultimately expressed in feet and inches, but the answers are not simply reducible to feet and inches. Instead, the answers represent various parameters of human experience in the same way that activity patterns do, and in order to successfully design your living spaces and the furniture in them, you must first discover these human dimensions and then use them as a guide for your designs.

Living Level

A further human parameter or dimension of your living space to consider in your furnishing of it is that of the *living level* i.e., the horizontal plane on which normal activities take place — talking, eating, sleeping, relaxing. Traditionally, most chairs, tables, desks, and beds have standard heights. More recently, however, there has been an influx of new furniture styles at nontraditional levels (e.g., platform beds, water beds, lofts, counters, cushions, pillows, and couches at floor level). Mixing traditional levels with these new levels can result in definite social and physical discomfort, as people try to talk to each other while occupying plateaus of varying heights.

Nor is it aesthetically pleasing to have your living area look like a haphazard collection of mountains and valleys. Both aesthetically and functionally, it makes sense to maintain some degree of uniformity in your space. This is not to say that you

Figure 1

cannot create certain areas and groupings at different levels, but rather that these different levels should fit functionally and aesthetically into the overall design of the space.

In figure 1 the individual chose to lower the entire level of his apartment—couches, tables, bed, etc.—giving the area a very spacious and uncluttered feeling and appearance. However, if one were to place a traditional-size chair, couch, or table into this grouping, it would give the appearance of Gulliver among the Lilliputians.

Division of Space

Space can be divided in a virtually limitless number of ways. In dividing it, the important questions are (1) how solid or porous is the division to be? (2) what use is the divider to serve other than division? and (3) what design will best enhance and contribute to the overall design of the space?

Division of space can best be seen as a spectrum of possibilities, ranging from solid walls to very minimal dividing units. A common space divider is illustrated in figures 150 and 151. It serves the purpose of separating the kitchen from the living room without the disadvantages of a solid barrier. It also offers additional uses—cabinets on the kitchen side and a counter that serves both sides.

An entirely different division of space is illustrated in figure 2. It separates the space in a more tangible way than the unit in figures 150 and 151 (page 181), yet it does so without the appearance of being bulky or heavy. It also possesses an intrinsic aesthetic appeal, particularly when the light streams through it and creates a light show of its own.

Figure 2

The division of space is often, correlatively, the creation of space. This is particularly important to keep in mind when you are confronted with a large space that you are trying to divide up into more human-size areas without partitioning it off into cubicles. The manner in which you choose to divide it will determine in large measure the nature of the space you are left to work with.

Modularity

The concept of modularity in furniture is one of relatively recent origins. Essentially, it refers to units whose parts can be (1) rearranged in different combinations, and (2) added to or subtracted from in order to change the size of the unit or vary its appearance. Units that allow for these operations naturally possess great flexibility. They make the task of customizing one's living space considerably easier and permit a much greater variety of possibilities. In addition, modularity adds to the average life expectancy of a piece of furniture, since it is so much more adaptable than traditional nonmodular units.

The large unit in figure 129 (page 165) is actually composed of four separate units bolted together. They can be separated and used individually or in various combinations, depending on the demands of the space at hand. Similarly, the wall unit pictured in figure 125 (page 160), is comprised of three independent sections.

The couches and tables in figure 1 (page 19) are all individual units that can be arranged in any number of different combinations.

Finally, figure 119 (page 155) shows another basic bookcase design that can be reduced or enlarged as the need arises.

In developing designs, it usually pays to try to make the units as modular as possible, and the resulting flexibility in design and multiplication of future possibilities makes the effort well worthwhile. This is not to say, however, that your furniture need necessarily *look* modular, as some contemporary pieces do but, rather, that they possess a *structural* modularity.

Woods and Stains

Another important aspect of the design of your furniture and your space as a whole involves your choice of woods and the stains (or lack of them) that you decide to finish them in. These are subjects that I will examine in some detail in subsequent chapters. For the present, I simply want to distinguish some basic "looks" you can create by varying woods and stains.

First, and most common among initiates in furniture construction, is the use of softwoods such as knotty pine and fir. These are the woods most available at lumberyards, and also the most inexpensive. When softwood is stained a medium or dark color such as walnut, the result is a somewhat rustic appearance, as you might expect to find in a cabin or hunting lodge.

Paradoxically, if pine and fir (and other light-colored woods) are not stained but are instead left in their natural state, they tend to take on a more contemporary or Scandinavian appearance. Natural wood also seems to have a natural aesthetic affinity for lots of sunlight and plants.

Special effects can be created by using artificially treated and distressed woods, like the Vermont barnboard in figure 150 (page 181). Although rustic in appearance, its rusticness is qualitatively different from common pine stained a color.

Finally, furniture can be constructed using fine-quality hardwoods such as oak, cherry, mahogany, maple, etc. Considerably more expensive than pine and other softwoods, pieces constructed with hardwoods take on the appearance of truly "fine furniture," exhibiting a richness and quality that cannot be equaled by cheaper substitutes.

To the question of whether these different effects can be satisfactorily combined in a single space, there is no simple answer. It depends in large measure upon the specific elements in each case. The chief danger comes in trying to mix fine-quality woods with the stained, rustic-looking softwoods. While they may look fine by themselves, softwoods tend to be outclassed by the rich quality of nature's finer products. (A more detailed study of hardwoods and softwoods will be considered in Chapter 2.)

Built-ins

Built-in furniture denotes furniture designed and constructed for a specific space. It has the advantage of getting the maximum functional use out of the space for which it is constructed. Since a customized, tailor-made piece of furniture so naturally fills up or fits into an existing space, thereby complementing it, it also has a pleasing and aesthetically satisfying appearance.

The advantages it possesses also constitute its disadvantages. By being built for a specific space, it often does not look good if it has to be moved to another space of different dimensions. This difficulty can at least be partially eliminated or assuaged if the units possess a modular design, which we discussed in the last section.

Figure 93 (page 137) shows a loft bed built into a specific space in the apartment. While the bed has a built-in appearance, however, the nature of the design is such that it can be used in a variety of different spaces, either as a loft or as a platform bed.

The unit in figure 102 (page 150) was built for the specific space it occupies in the photograph, but its tripartite modular design gives it great versatility for potential use in other spaces.

Summary

In this chapter I have tried to convey and illustrate the concepts and methods I find useful in designing furniture and arranging living spaces. I personally have a preference for designs with simple, clean lines, in which functional concerns are preeminent. However, I think that the elements we've examined are also relevant and useful to other types of design, to a greater or lesser degree.

Designs that possess relatively clean and simple lines have the added advantage of mixing well with other styles and forms of furniture, including antiques and traditional furniture. Generally speaking, the more complex, ornate, or idiosyncratic a design, the more difficulty it's going to have in aesthetically socializing with its roommates. And although too much homogeneity of furniture design can sometimes lead to an unexciting space, most people nevertheless strive for an overall harmony and unity of design in their living spaces. Failure in this regard can leave your place looking like an international smorgasbord instead of a unified expression of a distinct and unique human personality.

It's now time to turn from our speculative musings to the down-to-earth realm of sore thumbs and splinters. First we'll examine woods and materials, then construction methods, and finally staining and finishing techniques. We will then attempt to pull this all together in order to construct some interesting and useful pieces of furniture.

Trees and Wood

I find trees, and the lumber that comes from them, to be a truly impressive aspect of nature's creative handiwork. While growing, trees are complex, living organisms, utilizing an ingenious system of growth and development. As artistic natural objects, their forms and shapes are living sculptures, the colors of their foliage and textures of their bark more dazzling than any canvas. When they are cut, sawed, planed, and finished for manmade uses, we find that their external beauty is rivaled only by the concealed beauty of their interiors. Unlocked from its natural confines, the wood is displayed like treasure from a chest, a rich and spectacular collection of grains, colors, textures, and aromas in seemingly infinite variety.

Although there are a very large number of different species of trees in the world, there are a relatively small number of these that are used for building furniture, and an even smaller number that are commonly available at most lumberyards. Before going into a discussion of specific varieties — their characteristics, advantages and disadvantages, prices, etc. — let's consider first some general characteristics of all lumber.

General Characteristics of Wood

Lumber Types

All trees are divided into two basic types: *softwoods* and *hardwoods*. Softwood trees are evergreen trees, so named because they usually keep their foliage (usually green needles) all year long. Common types of softwoods are pines, firs, and spruces.

Hardwood trees are deciduous trees, which grow new foliage every spring (usually broad green leaves) and lose their foliage every fall after dressing in their brilliant autumn colors. Common types of hardwoods are oaks, maples, ashes, walnuts, and birches.

Lumber Sizing

The system of sizing for solid lumber is the source of much misunderstanding and confusion for people not familiar with the system. After all, there does not appear to be any logical reason why a 2"-by-4" board (commonly called, simply, 2 × 4) should actually measure only 1-1/2" by 3-1/2". The reason for this apparent paradox is due to the fact that the 2 × 4 designation represents the size of the lumber *after* it has been roughsawed from the tree, but *before* it has been dried (and thus shrunk) and *before* it has been planed smooth and true. The 2 × 4 preshrunk and preplaned dimension is thus referred to as the *nominal measurement,* and the 1-1/2 × 3-1/2 size is referred to as the *actual measurement.*

While most lumber purchased at lumberyards has been dried and planed, this is not always the case. The planing of the lumber, after it has been kiln-dried or air-dried, is referred to as *dressing* or *surfacing.* Thus, a piece of lumber that has been planed on all four sides is said to be "surfaced on four sides" and is designated with the notation *S4S.* If the top and bottom of the plank have been surfaced but not the edges, it is designated *S2S.* And if just the top of the plank is surfaced, it is referred to as *S1S.*

The history behind this double system of sizing is that there was a time when 2 × 4 referred to the actual, finished measurement of the lumber. However, over the years, lumbermen have found that in addition to increasing the price of lumber, they could further increase their profit by reducing the size of the product they were selling (in the same way that the size of candy bars has been gradually reduced while the price has risen). And while this inflationary technique has been very profitable for people selling lumber, it has made life that much more difficult for people buying it. A chart showing the nominal sizes and actual sizes of standard lumber appears at the end of this chapter (page 56).

Lumber Pricing

The price of a particular piece of lumber is determined by what *kind* of wood it is (pine, oak, etc.), what *grade* of wood it is (discussed later), and what *size* it is. The standard unit of measurement used in lumber pricing is known as a *board foot,* a term that designates the volume of lumber found in a board 1' × 1' × 1'' (figure 3). Using this as a standard unit, you can express the size of any piece of lumber in the number of board feet (abbreviated bd. ft.) it contains. The formula for this conversion is expressed as follows:

thickness of board in inches *multiplied by* width of board in feet *multiplied by* length of board in feet *equals* number of board feet.

For example, a board 1'' × 6'' × 8' contains 4 board feet ([1] × [1/2] × [8] = 4).

In addition to pricing lumber according to board feet, most lumberyards will also give you the price of your lumber in *linear feet*. This means that the price given will be for the particu-

Figure 3

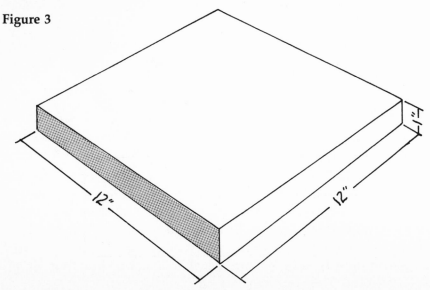

lar-size board you have in mind at a simple rate per foot. In other words, the lumberyard has already made the board-foot conversion for you and is expressing the price in terms of the specific-size board you are receiving. Thus, a board 1'' × 6'' × 8', which contains 4 board feet and sells for $0.60/bd. ft., will sell for $2.40. The linear-foot price of this board will thus be $.30/ft., and since it is 8' long, is again priced at $2.40.

When getting prices on lumber, securing a linear-foot price is helpful, since it gives you an immediate idea of how much you are going to be spending, without having to take the additional step of converting from board feet.

Grain

The *grain* of a board refers to the direction in which the wood fibers run. The grain direction is determined by the particular growth of the tree from which it was taken and the manner in which the board was sawed out of the tree at the mill. Since a board is a three-dimensional object, there are two basic grain parameters — the *horizontal plane,* along the length of the board; and the *vertical plane,* perpendicular to the horizontal plane (figure 4).

Figure 4

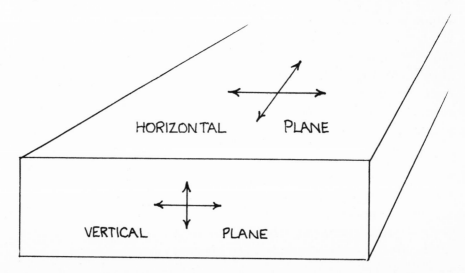

HORIZONTAL   PLANE

VERTICAL   PLANE

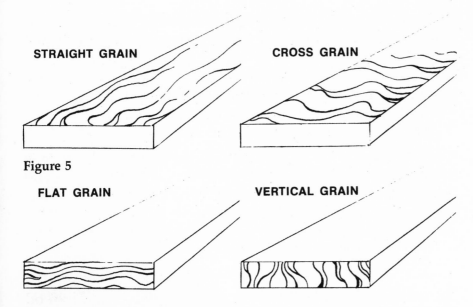

Figure 5

Figure 6

On the horizontal plane, a board is said to have *straight grain* when the grain runs parallel to the sides and *cross grain* when it runs perpendicular to the sides (figure 5). Straight-grained lumber is considerably stronger than cross-grained, and most boards are of this type.

On the vertical plane, a board is said to have *vertical grain* when the grain runs vertically up and down, and *flat grain* when it runs horizontally across (figure 6). Vertical-grained lumber is more susceptible to checks and splits (next section), and flat-grained lumber is more susceptible to warpage and shrinkage due to changes in moisture content. As for appearance, flat grain is considerably more interesting because it results from cutting across the growth rings, and in most woods it has a broad, swirling look. Vertical-grained wood has a much more uniform, lined appearance.

Special grain configurations are formed by taking boards from special parts of the tree. *Burl grain* results when boards are cut across certain kinds of knots in certain kinds of wood. *Crotch grain* is produced when a board is sawed across the divergence of two or more main members of the tree.

Moisture Content of Lumber

Lumber freshly sawed from trees is termed *green lumber*. Such lumber has a very substantial moisture content, as it contains considerable quantities of both water and sap. In order to be suitable for furniture (or building) construction, it is essential that this lumber be thoroughly dried before it is used. In days gone by, lumber was dried by a method known as *air drying:* Boards were stacked in piles with levels separated by slats to allow for air circulation on all four sides. This method is still used occasionally, but the length of time required for complete drying (at least a year) has caused it to be replaced in large measure by *kiln drying,* a process during which lumber is subjected to extreme heat in a kiln (oven).

If lumber is used for furniture (or other) construction when it is not completely dry, the natural expansion and contraction of the wood as it dries will cause it to split, check, warp, and bow. Always insist on dry lumber, preferably kiln-dried (this will be stamped on the ends or sides of the boards in most cases). The latter is all that the vast majority of lumberyards stock.

In the case of *construction-grade lumber* — 2 × 4 through 2 × 12 fir and spruce — the stamp *kiln-dried* is often not sufficient guarantee that the lumber is thoroughly dry, particularly when the lumber is stored outside. It pays to check it out yourself, and you can do this by comparing the weights of equal-size boards (wet boards are considerably heavier). Or if you have the space and the time to wait, you can insure their dryness by air-drying them yourself.

Virtually all *nonconstruction* softwoods and hardwoods at reputable yards are kiln-dried and thoroughly dry as well.

Lumber Defects

Lumber is susceptible to a number of different sorts of defects (that is, defects from man's standpoint, not nature's). The relative presence or absence of these defects helps determine the grade of the lumber (see the next section on lumber grading) and thus helps determine the cost of the lumber. In selecting the lumber for your project, the nature of the project will pretty much determine which defects are acceptable and which are unacceptable for your use. Some people actually seek out lumber with defects for a certain appearance they are trying to create, for example, a rustic "knotty pine" look or a weathered and distressed "barn siding" look.

Defects fall into several general categories, and it pays to become familiar with each of them.

Knots

Knots are the most familiar defect found in wood. Knots are actually those places on the main trunk where branches diverged and grew out. Knots are very hard and are difficult to saw through. There are two basic types of knots—*tight knots*, which are a firm and solid part of the wood surrounding them, and *loose knots*, which have become detached from the wood surrounding them and are apt to fall out (if they haven't already done so). Loose knots can be glued back into place if they do fall out.

Knots can be painted over with no particular difficulty, provided they are sealed with a coat of shellac or varnish to prevent their resin from *bleeding* through. Knots also pose no problem in staining and finishing, provided you don't mind their appearance.

Because they represent an interruption and change of direction in the wood grain, knots tend to weaken a board. This is normally not a critical factor unless the board is going to be put under a great deal of stress, or unless the size or number of knots is excessive.

When laying out your lumber, avoid placing knots on the joints, as they are very difficult to nail, screw, or cut grooves into. In addition, the cutting of a knot increases the likelihood that it will fall out.

Checks, Shakes, Splits

After knots, the most distinctive category of defects in lumber is the separations in the lumber that normally, though not always, occur at the ends of boards. There are three main types (figure 7A): *Checks* are separations in the wood across the growth rings that do not extend all the way through the board; *splits* are separations across the growth rings that extend all the way through the board; *shakes* are separations that occur between the growth rings.

Although these three defects normally occur at the ends of boards in the process of kiln-drying or sitting on the shelves at the lumberyard, they can also occur on the ends formed after you have cut a board, particularly if the board is not thoroughly dry. As I have already mentioned, it is essential that you use the dryest wood available for your projects.

As far as using wood with these defects is concerned, I've always felt that these defects are not worth attempting to repair by filling or gluing and clamping, unless they occur after you have completed your project. Wood that has already started to split, check, or shake will tend to continue to do so along the same lines unless the damaged portions have been cut off and discarded. There's no sense in taking a chance with the quality of your finished project to save a few cents. And if you are careful about the wood you select from the lumberyard, you won't be faced with these problems very often.

Figure 7A

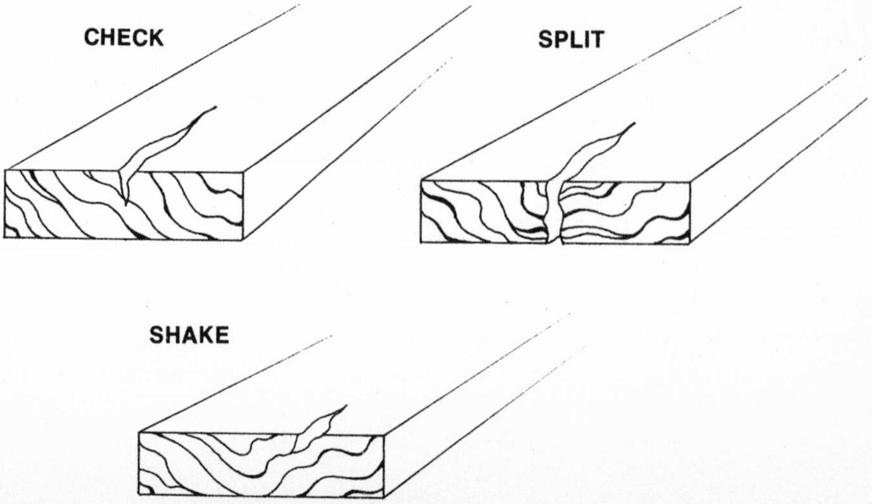

CHECK   SPLIT

SHAKE

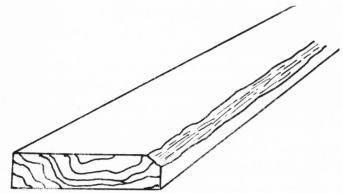

Figure 7B

When cutting off the offending portions, try to cut an inch or two beyond the actual separation to make sure you've removed all the wood with separation tendencies. It's a little like a dentist removing decay from a tooth: You don't want to take a chance on leaving any behind.

A further problem to be on the lookout for is the presence of bark (and absence of wood) on the edges or corners of a board, a condition known as "wane" (figure 7B). These defective edges are usually rounded or slanted instead of square, as they represent the outside surface of the log from which the board was cut. Unless the edge is to be concealed or sawn off in reducing the board to a smaller size, boards with this defect should not be accepted.

Bowing, Twisting, Crooking, Cupping

One of the more frustrating aspects of woodworking is having to deal with wood that is not straight or flat. The terms which designate the various lumber defects in this area are *bowing, twisting, crooking,* and *cupping,* as illustrated in figure 8A.

These defects are the result of either improper drying or the natural reactions of a board to changes in moisture and temperature after it has been dried. In any case, avoid selecting boards like these at all costs.

To spot bows, twists, and crooks, pick the board up off the ground at one end, turn it on its edge, and sight down along its length. If there's any doubt, flip the board over and sight down along the other edge, or simply lay the board on a flat surface.

To locate cupped boards, place the end of the board at eye level or lay a straightedge across the width of the board. Do this to both ends, as often one end will differ from the other.

Don't worry if you feel a little self-conscious at first in scrutinizing the boards this way; after a little practice, it will seem perfectly natural.

Figure 8A

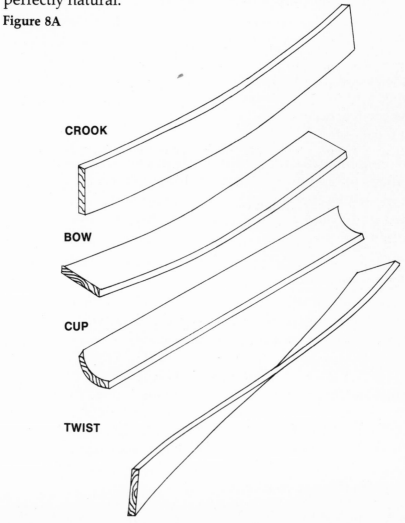

CROOK

BOW

CUP

TWIST

Sometimes, bends and twists in boards occur after you have purchased the lumber. To minimize the chance of this happening, always store lumber lying down flat (not standing up) and support it along its entire length. Try to keep it in a place that has a relatively constant temperature and humidity, and never store it outside where it will be exposed to the elements.

If you find yourself with defective boards (and with softwoods such as pine, this is not uncommon even if you take precautions), you can still work with the boards if the defects are not too severe. The secret lies in the joints. For example, if you are making bookshelves with dado joints, save your bowed, twisted, and cupped members for the shelves. Assemble the frame with the grooves already cut, then simply knock the shelves into place, using a piece of scrap wood as a buffer between the hammer and shelf to avoid damaging the wood. The dado grooves will actually straighten the board out, provided the fit is not too loose.

If you are joining boards in butt or flush joints, the secret is to use clamps to hold the pieces tightly together, and then secure the joint with screws or glue. Nails normally won't hold a warped or twisted board in position after the clamps have been removed.

Avoid using warped and twisted boards for other more advanced joints (such as miters or mortise and tenon) or along large spans (even though the ends are straightened out, the middle will remain warped or twisted) or for cutting grooves into (the groove will not be a uniform depth).

Pitch Pockets

The final defect to keep an eye out for is called *pitch pockets*, which are found normally in certain softwoods, namely spruce, pine, and Douglas fir. They have the appearance of long, narrow open wounds in the wood; they are orange in color, and they often ooze a very sticky substance called *pitch*, a resin found in the tree (figure 8B).

Using boards with pitch pockets in visible places on your piece

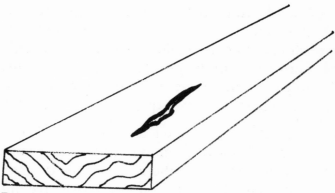

Figure 8B

should be avoided. They are messy to work around and difficult to clean and fill, as the pitch tends to bleed through whatever filling you use. If using it is unavoidable, clean it out as best you can with turpentine. It also helps to take a chisel and remove as much of the discolored area as you can. Seal the cavity with shellac or varnish, then fill and finish.

Lumber Grading

Lumber is classified or graded according to the number of defects (or lack of them) it has. Hardwoods and softwoods have different systems of grading. For hardwoods, the first two grades are termed *firsts* and *seconds,* both of which are relatively free of blemishes. These two categories are normally combined into a single category, *FAS* (firsts and seconds), and it is this grade that is generally available at most lumberyards. The lower grades range from *thirds* to *#3B common* and are normally available only on special request. Additionally, both sides, or *faces,* are graded individually. Thus if a board is graded *FAS 1 face,* it means that only one side will be top quality. Most of the hardwoods at lumberyards are *FAS 2 face* (that is, both sides are top quality).

The top grade for softwoods is termed *#1 and #2 clear.* This grade requires that the boards have no knots or defects. The next grade is *#1 common,* a category that permits a small number of tight knots. *#2 common* permits a few more tight knots but is still quite suitable for use in pine furniture. *#3 common* allows loose knots, some of which may have already fallen out. It is normally unsuitable for wood that will be visible. The bottom grades, *#4 common* and *#5 common,* are completely unsuitable.

Most lumberyards carry clear grades and also #1 and #2 common mixed together. Occasionally #3 common is available, but while the difference in price between clear and #1 and #2 common is substantial (often over 50 percent) the difference in price between #2 common and #3 common is not sufficient to warrant the latter's use for furniture construction except in unusual circumstances (e.g., shelves which will not show). For furniture that will ultimately be painted, #2 common (generally referred to simply as #2) is more than adequate, once the knots have been sealed, filled, and sanded. Figure 8C is a chart summarizing softwood and hardwood grades.

Figure 8C   *Hardwood Grading*

Firsts and Seconds (FAS)	Both sides relatively free of blemishes
Select	One side relatively free of blemishes
#1 Common	Short widths and narrow lengths
#2 and #3 Common	Unsuitable for furniture making

Softwood Grading

#1 and #2 Clear	No knots or defects
#1 and #2 Common	Small number of tight knots
#3 Common	Some loose knots (unsuitable for visible surfaces)
#4 and #5 Common	Unsuitable for furniture making

Plywood and Veneer

Plywood and Veneer Construction

The term *plywood* designates sheets of wood that are formed by laminating together a number of thin layers that have been peeled from the tree and glued together. The plywood sheets that result can vary in thickness from 1/8'' to 1-1/8'' and are available in 1/8'' intervals (although 3/4'' is the largest size most yards commonly stock). Standard-size sheets are 4' × 8', although larger sizes are available.

There are three basic types of plywood, classified according to their interior construction (figure 9). *Veneer*, or *standard*, plywood refers to sheets constructed of a number of thin layers (the exact number, from three to seven, depends on the overall thickness of the sheet) with the outer two sides consisting of 1/28'' face veneer. *Lumber core* has a fairly thick solid wood core with a 1/16'' layer on either side and a 1/28'' face veneer. *Particleboard core* has a core of treated and compressed mixture of wood particles and glue. This type also has two veneer face sheets on each side the standard 1/28'' thickness. For cabinetry and furniture, lumber-core plywood is far superior to work with, since the few layers make the edges much easier to handle.

Plywood is further divided into the categories of hardwoods and softwoods, depending upon which sort of veneer facing it has. Softwood plywood is usually faced with Douglas fir and is graded on a scale running *N, A, B, C,* and *D*—these letters representing the quality of the face sheets (N is perfect, A permits a few corrected imperfections, and on down the scale in terms of quality). Each side is graded individually; for example, the best softwood plywood most lumberyards stock is *A-C*, which signifies that it is good on one side and moderately poor on the other. For any surface that is going to be exposed, nothing lower than A should be used. If the plywood is going to be exposed to the elements, you should specify plywood laminated with *exterior glue*, as ordinary glue will not withstand the elements and will result in the layers becoming delaminated.

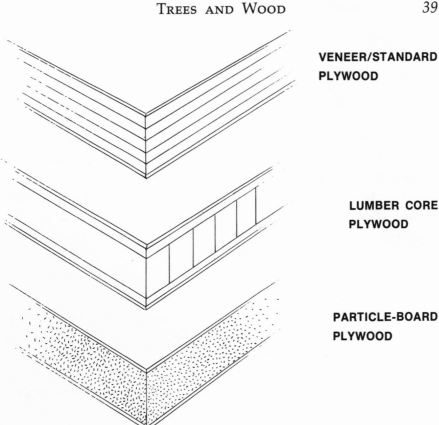

VENEER/STANDARD
PLYWOOD

LUMBER CORE
PLYWOOD

PARTICLE-BOARD
PLYWOOD

Figure 9

Hardwood plywood is generally available in birch, oak, mahogany, ash, walnut, cherry, and maple. Other more exotic veneer plywoods are sometimes available, and you can always purchase the veneer separately from a special mail-order house and glue it onto a piece of standard plywood yourself.

Hardwood plywood is somewhat more expensive than standard softwood plywood, but it is infinitely preferable for furniture. Like softwood plywood, hardwood plywood is also graded according to the quality of each of its faces. The scale runs from *specialty grade (SP)*, which is made to order, *premium grade (#1)*, *good grade* (also *#1*), sound grade (*#2*), utility grade (*#3*), and *backing grade (#4)*. Again, any face sheet in your project that is going to be visible should not be rated below #1.

Most hardwood veneers are laminated onto lumber-core bodies, enabling you to work with edges almost as if they were solid wood. In the case of softwood, the multilayer standard, or veneer, plywood is more common.

Advantages and Disadvantages

Although I've always had a preference for solid lumber, there is no doubt that plywood and veneers have an indispensable place in furniture construction. As a matter of fact, in the eighteenth and nineteenth centuries, veneering was a highly prized art, and most of the fine furniture was made using veneers extensively (legs, spindles, trim, etc., were solid woods naturally). During this period, furniture constructed entirely of solid woods was for the most part considered to be of inferior quality and was found mainly in rural and lower-income homes.

Around the end of the nineteenth century and the beginning of this century, solid-oak furniture became quite popular and was sold in large quantities through the Sears Roebuck Company as well as many other smaller companies. This "turn-of-the-century oak" is currently enjoying quite a revival of popular interest.

Today, virtually all wood furniture is wood veneer or, worse, synthetic veneer, the latter colored and grained to resemble real wood. The major exception is the "Early American" line of furniture, made for the most part of solid knotty pine. Top-quality wood furniture in solid hardwoods is available, but it is difficult to find and often quite expensive.

There are a number of distinct advantages to using plywood, which is faced with veneer. First, plywoods come in large sheets (the standard size is 4' × 8', and larger sheets are available on request). These sheets enable you to use a single piece of wood for those large pieces that your furniture frequently requires — doors, tops, backs, sides, etc. Since the widest standard width that solid lumber comes in is 12'' (the actual dimension may range from 11-1/4'' to 11-1/2''), anything wider than that involves gluing individual boards together.

Second, due to its unique construction — the grain of each layer is perpendicular to the grain of the layer above and the layer below it—plywood is somewhat more resistant to warpage than solid lumber for free-swinging and free-hanging pieces like doors and adjustable shelves. This is not to say that plywood absolutely won't warp, but it is more resistant.

Third, using plywood with a hardwood veneer face is by and large more economical than using solid hardwood, since the actual hardwood used for the veneer is only a 1/28''-thick layer on either side of the sheet instead of solid through and through. The method used in taking the veneer off the tree—it's peeled off similarly to unrolling a roll of paper towels—is also a much more economical use of the tree. Cutting solid-wood planks out of a tree results in a considerable amount of wasted wood, not counting all the wood on the inside of the board that may never show. As a result, you normally pay considerably less per square foot for plywood than for solid wood.

Fourth, these same veneer processes that so tremendously increase the yield of trees mean that there is a larger variety of woods available in veneers than in solid woods. This is particularly apparent with rare woods from exotic places, such as teak, rosewood, zebrawood. Even when these woods are available in solid form, the cost is normally prohibitive for any large-scale projects.

On the other hand, there are some definite disadvantages to using veneer-faced plywoods instead of solid woods. First, while plywoods come in large sheets, the largest standard thickness is 3/4'', although some lumber-core veneer-faced plywoods can be had as thick as 1-1/8''. Most solid-lumber softwoods and many solid-lumber hardwoods are available in sizes up to (and greater than) 4'' × 4'', and even larger in the cases of cedar, redwood, pine, and fir.

Second, since the veneer is only 1/28'' thick, there is a definite limitation to the sanding, planing, and other kinds of wood shaping that can be done to it—particularly important when fitting joints.

Third, due again to its thinness, the wear and tear the veneer shows is likely to be unflattering, particularly if it cracks or chips off. Chipping off is also a problem when cutting plywoods, particularly on crosscuts across the grain and on corners. And once veneer cracks, splits, or chips, it's fairly difficult to repair satisfactorily. By contrast, solid wood actually increases in beauty as it ages, its imperfections giving it its distinctive character without the worry of exposing the reality that lurks beneath the surface of veneer-faced plywoods.

Fourth, the edges of plywood pieces pose a very serious problem. Since they are not covered by the veneer facing, they reveal a cross-section of the different layers that make up the plywood sheet. Thus, they have to be concealed in some way, and there are several techniques for solving this to various degrees of satisfaction. Edges can be mitered (figure 11); or they can be butted on their inside edges, with a piece of quar-

Figure 10

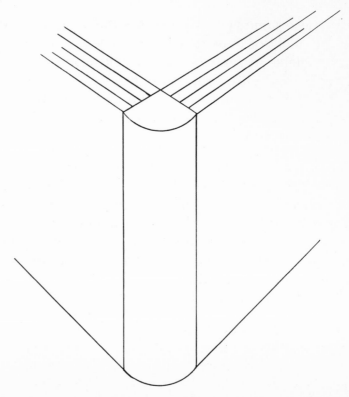

ter-round molding filling the gap they create (figure 10); also resin-backed wood-veneer tape (figure 12) or solid-wood molding (figure 13) can be glued on. Each of these solutions has certain advantages and disadvantages, and the particular situation will dictate which is most appropriate.

Fifth, veneers simply don't seem to give the same feeling of depth and texture that solid woods do. As solid woods age, they develop a very distinctive and beautiful patina, which veneers simply cannot duplicate. The grain pattern on veneers is also usually substantially different from solid woods due to the way it is peeled from the tree (although this is not always a disadvantage).

Finally, while veneers are ideal for inlay work, they are obviously inappropriate for engraving, carving, or turning. For these operations, solid wood must be employed.

Figure 11

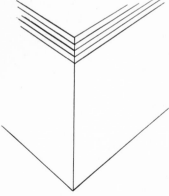

Figure 12   **Figure 13**

Thus, both solid woods and veneer-faced plywoods have their respective advantages and disadvantages. Certain projects may require one, other projects may require the other; in most cases, however, you'll find that a judicious use of both is the most intelligent course to steer.

Solid Lumber

Although the advantages we noted of using veneers are un-deniable—cost economy, large sheet size, resistance to warp-age—working with solid lumber is really the essence of woodworking. The knowledge that the plank you are shaping, jointing, sanding, and finishing was a piece of wood taken directly from a tree, that its rings represent the winters and summers it endured, its knots the branches that arched from its trunk, provides you with a special relationship to that piece of wood. That piece of wood, with its shape and size, texture and color, grain pattern and imperfections, is different from any other piece of wood in nature. Working with wood in this fashion gives you the feeling of touching something once alive, whose existence you will transform and preserve, displaying its beauty for all to see.

Though sheets of veneer plywood are still wood, they are the product of modern technology—peeled off the tree in giant rolls like skin off an onion, its layers laminated under great pressure, sliced up into uniform-size sheets with uniform appearance. Working a piece of wood produced in this fashion simply does not provide the same quality of feeling or sense of relationship that you get with solid woods. This lack of feeling is only reinforced when you realize the impossibility of carving, turning, planing, and shaping the piece of wood in front of you for fear of turning the princely appearance of its face sheet into the froglike reality of its interior; this feeling is exacerbated by the frustration of working with its coarse and layered edges.

This is not to say that veneer is not useful or necessary for many furniture projects; as we noted, the most intelligent approach is the judicious combination of both veneers and hardwoods. The point being made is simply that for me, the real joy and essence of woodworking lies in the experience of fashioning and preserving the spirit and existence of the trees from which my material was derived, creating and sculpting new forms of natural beauty that will endure.

Hardwood and Softwoods

We have already noted the distinction between hardwoods and softwoods — hardwoods designating lumber derived from deciduous trees, softwoods referring to the lumber from evergreens.

As its name implies, lumber from hardwood trees is usually of greater hardness than lumber from softwood trees, although there are exceptions to this, for instance, balsa, which is a "soft" hardwood. By and large, however, the two terms are generally accurate descriptions of the members of their groups.

Most softwood trees grow at a much more rapid rate than most hardwood trees. As a result, softwood lumber is in much greater supply than hardwood lumber and is also obviously much cheaper as a result. Virtually all lumber used in house and building construction today is softwood. Much of the furniture made today is also made of softwoods, especially painted and "Early American" styles. In building construction, hardwoods are reserved for floors, cabinets, and some trim. Hardwoods are used in the construction of fine furniture and in the important support members (i.e., legs) of less expensive furniture.

Softwoods thus have the advantages of being cheaper, more readily available, and easier to work with. They have the disadvantages of being fairly soft and thus lacking in durability and strength. They nick and scar easily and are more susceptible to warpage and shrinkage. The texture, grain, and coloring of finished softwoods is also inferior to that of most fine hardwoods.

Hardwoods are relatively expensive and much less readily available than softwoods but are strong, durable, and much more resistant to warpage and shrinkage. When properly finished, they take on beauty and richness that simply cannot be duplicated.

In addition to availability, price, and size, the relevant categories for evaluating wood involve color or tint, grain type, grain pattern, hardness and strength, and workability.

Availability

Although there are quite a large number of solid hardwoods that are suitable for making furniture, there are relatively few that are readily available and stocked by your local yard. These usually include oak, maple, and lauan (Philippine mahogany). Less common but still normally available by special order or at select lumberyards are woods like ash, birch, cherry, Honduras mahogany, poplar, and walnut. More rare still and usually available only at specialty yards are woods like beech, teak, rosewood, and zebrawood. One special hardwood item that is readily available and that is extremely useful is butcherblock. Butcherblock is comprised of a series of narrow 1''- to 2''-wide strips of hardwood—usually maple, sometimes pecan or oak or another hardwood—laminated together under intense pressure. It is then sanded level and oiled. It has the advantage of providing virtually any size sheet of solid hardwood 1'' to 2'' thick at a price reasonably affordable. It is invaluable for desk tops, counter tops, and workbenches, and it is featured in a number of the projects in this book.

To a certain extent, lumber availability does depend on your geographical location. In areas that grow certain species for lumber production, those particular types are likely to be ready at hand and also cheaper. In almost all cases, however, there should be one or more yards in your area that specialize in hardwoods and that can order whatever woods they don't stock. Of course, it's always preferable to examine the specific wood you are buying before committing your money, but this isn't always possible, particularly for the more exotic woods. And if there are unjustifiable defects in the wood, most yards won't expect you to take it even on a special order.

To locate the yards in your area that deal in hardwoods may require you to do a little detective work. The best way to begin is by checking the yellow pages of your telephone directory or asking at the yard you normally do business with. Be prepared for a lot of negative responses, however, because most yards simply don't bother with hardwoods; their operations are geared more for the home handyman and contractor than for the makers of fine furniture. Don't become discouraged, however, for after a while, you will ferret out those places that talk hardwood language, a dialect much different from that spoken at most neighborhood yards.

Price

Geographical location is again a determining factor in the case of lumber prices. In those areas that grow and mill certain types of trees, prices should naturally be lower for those types. In addition to this sort of price variation, prices also vary *within* a geographical area, often drastically, and it pays to check out all of the places in your area on *each species* of wood. Of course, the quality of the lumber varies from place to place also, and these differences can only be learned by firsthand apprasal. The type of service also varies from yard to yard, and it makes a big difference whether you are allowed to help select the lumber you are buying or have to take what you are given.

Size

Although we have already spoken about lumber sizing in general, there is one added sizing factor in the case of hardwoods: Many of them are available only in *random widths* and *random lengths* (abbreviated *RW* and *RL*). The reason for this is that milling and cutting lumber down to standard widths and standard lengths involves considerable waste, and the scarcity and value of hardwood discourage lumbermen from witnessing this waste going onto the scrap pile. Those species commonly stocked by local yards, such as oak, maple, and lauan, are usually available in standard widths, but other less common varieties are always sold on the basis of random width and random length. This simply means that you have to figure out the specific sizes you need for your project and then try to match up the existing stock as closely as you can with your materials list in order to minimize waste at your end. Many yards will cut longer boards down provided the remaining piece is not too short (and hence unsalable).

Natural Color

Surprisingly enough, most woods in their natural state are very difficult to distinguish on the basis of color alone, as many exhibit a common cream or off-white color. This is surprising to most people when they first discover it because we have come to identify woods with their stained and finished hues. It is true that red oak has a reddish tint, cherry a slight pinkish tint, and so on. By and large, however, most woods can be stained most colors; for example, cherry can easily take a nice brown walnut stain, oak a cherry stain, and pine a mahogany stain. We will examine this subject further in Chapter 4. This note is only to prepare you for the surprise you might otherwise experience when the yardman pulls a piece of natural oak out of the rack and you discover that it doesn't look like the table or bed that you have back home.

Grain Type

Hardwoods are said to be either *open-grained* or *close-grained*. Open-grained woods, such as oak, are characterized by longitudinal striations and miniature crevices, which give the wood surface an overall uneven texture. If you run your fingernail across the grain of an unfinished piece of open-grained wood, you can feel the ridges. Close-grained woods, such as maple or cherry, are just the opposite. The surface of the wood is smooth and even and can be finished to a mirrorlike luster. In order to achieve this smooth texture on open-grained woods, it is necessary to treat them with a wood filler (Chapter 4).

Grain Pattern

The grain pattern of a particular piece of lumber depends on what type of wood it is and just how it was taken from the tree. When the board was *plain-sawed* across the growth rings, it is said to exhibit a V-shaped *flat grain*. When the board was *quarter-sawed* from the tree, it is said to exhibit a *straight grain* or *edge grain*. These different types of grain were discussed earlier in the chapter (page 29).

Wood grain also varies from wood to wood, reflecting the different ways the trees grow. The best way to learn to distinguish and recognize different grain types is to compare them with one another in both natural and finished states.

Hardness and Strength

The hardness and strength of a piece of wood are proportionate to the density of the cells and fibers of the wood. Most hardwoods are fairly dense and as a result are quite strong. Although the hardest wood is probably the fairly exotic lignum vitae, common hardwoods such as oak, cherry, birch, mahogany, and especially maple are very hard and very strong. However, some so-called hardwoods, such as balsa and poplar, are neither hard nor strong and are therefore more like the majority of softwoods, whose cell and fiber structures are on the whole much less dense. On the other hand, there are some softwoods, such as fir and redwood, that rank moderately high in the categories of hardness and strength. All of which is really to say that it pays to know the characteristics of the specific woods you are considering and the particular uses that they can best be put to.

Workability

Although "hard" hardwoods are more difficult to saw, chisel, and plane than softer woods, they are a joy to work with if your tools are sharp and (if you are working with hand tools) time is not a critical factor. (There is little time difference if you are using power tools.) Because of their hardness, hardwoods hold very sharp edges, can be worked to close tolerances, and lend themselves to intricate carving and inlay. And of course the big payoff for working with these sorts of woods lies in their durability in withstanding the vicissitudes of time, accidents, and careless guests and children, as well as in the rich and natural beauty they exhibit.

Softwoods are naturally much easier to work with hand tools, but they do not hold an edge or join nearly as well as "hard" hardwoods.

Wood Glossary

Listed below are brief descriptions of the woods you are most likely to come into contact with. Unfortunately, any description such as this is a poor substitute for actually seeing and working with the woods firsthand, but it will give you some idea of their basic strengths and weaknesses.

Ash, white *(Fraxinus americana)*
Location — eastern half of U.S.
Color and grain — creamy through grayish colors; straight grain and open pores
Characteristics — heavy, strong, stiff, shock-resistant, tough; excellent bending properties; easy to work with power tools
Uses — baseball bats, tool handles, oars, bentwood furniture parts

Basswood *(Tilia americana)*
Location — eastern half of U.S. and Canada

Color and grain — creamy white to creamy brown; small pores, faint growth rings
Characteristics — lightweight hardwood; weak, moderately stiff, low in shock resistance; easy to work with hand tools
Uses — cores for lumber-core plywood, crates, builders' mill-work

Beech, American *(Fagus grandifolia)*
Location — eastern half of U.S.
Color and grain — white with reddish to reddish brown tint; tiny pores
Characteristics — heavy, strong, shock-resistant; good bending properties
Uses — furniture, cooperage, veneers, railroad ties

Birch, yellow *(Betula alleghaniensis)*
Location — eastern half of U.S. and Canada
Color and grain — creamy to light reddish brown; tiny pores
Characteristics — hard, heavy, strong, stiff, high shock resistance; machines and works well with power tools
Uses — furniture, veneers, general millwork

Cherry, black *(Prunus serotina)*
Location — Maine to South Dakota; south along the Appalachians
Color and grain — creamy light tan to dark reddish brown; tiny individual pores, but groupings form distinctive patterns that are visible
Characteristics — moderately heavy and hard, stiff, strong, shock-resistant; machines and works well with power tools
Uses — furniture, caskets, woodenware, finish trim

Chestnut *(Castanea dentata)*
Location — eastern U.S. (quite rare now due to chestnut blight in early 1900s)
Color and grain — reddish brown; open pores, coarse texture, straight-grained; available now mostly as "wormy" chestnut, exhibiting small holes dotting the surface, which are the result of borers in the blighted wood

Characteristics—moderately hard, stiff, and strong; easy to work with hand or power tools
Uses—furniture, veneer paneling

Elm, American *(Ulmus americana)*
Location—eastern U.S.
Color and grain—light to dark brown; tiny pores visible as wavy lines on end grains, lighter than the background wood
Characteristics—moderately heavy, hard, stiff but weak, good shock resistance; good bending qualities
Uses—furniture, veneers, bentwood parts

Fir, Douglas *(Pseudotsuga menziesii)*—not a true fir
Location—Pacific and Rocky Mountain states
Color and grain—white through yellowish through red; prominent and abundant resin canals; "wild" grain with strong differences in texture
Characteristics—very stiff, moderately heavy, hard, strong, and shock-resistant; works fairly easily with hand or power tools when thoroughly dry
Uses—general construction timbers and plywood, general millwork

Hickory *(Carya)*
Location—most of eastern U.S.
Color and grain—brown to reddish brown; visible pores that are often filled with tyloses, (frothy, waterproof material)
Characteristics—very heavy, hard, strong, stiff, and shock-resistant; overall the toughest commercial wood
Uses—tool handles, athletic equipment, furniture

Mahogany, Cuban *(Swietenia mahogani);* **Honduras mahogany** *(Swietenia macrophylla);* **African mahogany** *(Khaya ivorensis)*
Locations—West Indies, Central America, and equatorial Africa, respectively
Color and grain—pale to deep reddish brown, becoming darker on exposure to light; open, diffuse pores; distinctive "ripple marks"; unusual grain patterns available (crotch, fiddleback, mottle, plain stripe)

Characteristics—moderate density and hardness; machines, carves, and works very well with hand and power tools
Uses—fine furniture, boat construction

Mahogany, Philippine *(Shorea)*—red lauan, white lauan, tanguile, etc., which are not true mahoganies but, rather, Philippine hardwoods with the appearance of mahogany, though coarser in texture
Location—Philippines
Color and grain—light tan to dark reddish brown; open, diffuse pores
Characteristics—moderate density and hardness; similar to true mahoganies, but stringier and coarser in texture and general appearance; works well with hand or power tools
Uses—furniture, boat construction

Maple, sugar *(Acer saccharum)*
Location—eastern half of U.S., especially Northeast
Color and grain—cream to light reddish brown; tiny pores; unusual grain patterns available (curly, fiddleback, blister figures)
Characteristics—extremely hard, strong, stiff, dense, shock-resistant; machines and works well with power tools
Uses—furniture, flooring, bowling alleys, woodenware, butcherblocks, and counters

Oak, American *(Quercus)*—white oak *(Q. alba)* and red oak *(Q. borealis)*
Location—eastern U.S.
Color and grain—cream to light reddish brown; open grain with large pores, pores of white oak filled with tyloses, a waterproof substance; large, distinctive light-reflecting rays
Characteristics—very heavy, hard, strong, stiff, durable; machines and works well with power tools
Uses—furniture, flooring, caskets, boat construction, millwork, woodenware

Pine, white *(Pinus)*—eastern white pine *(P. strobus)*, also called punkin pine, and western white pine *(P. monticola)*

Location — eastern and western U.S.

Color and grain — cream to light reddish brown; visible resin canals

Characteristics — soft, moderately light, stiff, and low in shock resistance; works well with hand or power tools

Uses — furniture, construction, millwork

Poplar, yellow *(Liriodendron tulipifera)* — not a true poplar

Location — eastern U.S.

Color and grain — brownish yellow with greenish tinge; tiny pores; straight-grained

Characteristics — light to medium weight, moderately soft, stiff, and low in shock resistance; it works well with hand or power tools

Uses — furniture, pulpwood, musical instruments, crates

Redwood *(Sequoia sempervirens)*

Location — north of San Francisco to Oregon in California fog belt

Color and grain — deep, reddish brown; alternating glossy and dull textures

Characteristics — moderately hard, stiff, strong, fair shock resistance; excellent decay and termite resistance; easy to work with hand or power tools

Uses — construction, millwork, siding, outdoor furniture, and decks

Rosewood, Brazilian *(Dalbergia nigra)*

Location — Brazil

Color and grain — light to dark browns, with purple and black streaks; fairly large pores

Characteristics — very heavy, hard, stiff, strong; works well with power tools

Uses — fine furniture, musical instruments, veneers

Teak *(Tectona grandis)*

Location — Burma, eastern India, Indochina, Java

Color and grain — tan through light brown, with light and dark streaks

Characteristics — hard, stiff, strong, good shock resistance; works and machines well with power tools
Uses — fine furniture, veneers, boat construction, flooring

Walnut, American *(Juglans nigra)*
Location — Midwest and eastern U.S.
Color and grain — light to chocolate brown; visible pores appear as dark grooves and streaks; many unusual grain configurations
Characteristics — very hard, stiff, strong, good shock resistance; machines, carves, and works well with power tools and hand tools
Uses — fine furniture, paneling, gunstocks

Standard Dimensions of Finished Lumber

Nominal Size	*Actual Size*
1 × 2	3/4'' × 1-1/2''
1 × 3	3/4'' × 2-1/2''
1 × 4	3/4'' × 3-1/2''
1 × 6	3/4'' × 5-1/2''
1 × 8	3/4'' × 7-1/4''
1 × 10	3/4'' × 9-1/4''
1 × 12	3/4'' × 11-1/4''
2 × 2	1-1/2'' × 1-1/2''
2 × 3	1-1/2'' × 2-1/2''
2 × 4	1-1/2'' × 3-1/2''
2 × 6	1-1/2'' × 5-1/2''
2 × 8	1-1/2'' × 7-1/4''
2 × 10	1-1/2'' × 9-1/4''
2 × 12	1-1/2'' × 11-1/4''

NOTE: The thicknesses of 3'' and 4'' lumber are the same as the respective widths above. The thickness of 5/4'' lumber is 1-1/8''. (The respective widths are the same as above.)

Construction Methods

Once you have determined the design of your piece of furniture and have selected the materials that you want, you are ready to get down to the real hard-core aspects of furniture construction. Working with wood is an extremely logical process, comprised of a series of predetermined steps that must be taken in a certain sequential order. Woodworking is not the sort of thing that you "play by ear," relying on bursts of ingenuity to extricate yourself from the hole you've put yourself into. Therefore, it is absolutely essential that you *take your time* in planning and executing your projects. Many of the steps, once taken, are irreversible and cannot be easily corrected, if at all, without starting anew. People who are always looking for shortcuts and fail to adequately anticipate the future consequences of their actions will quickly find themselves in the "boat in the basement" predicament (or its equivalent) when it comes to making fine furniture.

The first step in the process of construction is the making of a diagram.

Making a Diagram

Drawing a diagram of your proposed project accomplishes a number of important functions. First, it gets the ball rolling for your project by forcing you to put all the ideas you've been considering down in concrete terms, substituting specific dimensions for general concepts. Since some people spend a lifetime making plans that are never carried out, the importance of this initial step should not be underestimated.

Second, making a diagram gives you a plan to work with, a blueprint for all the future steps. You will find yourself referring back to it again and again as you make specific decisions regarding the construction of your project.

Third, it helps you visualize what the finished piece is going to look like. Most of us have difficulty in imagining what something will look like in the flesh if all we've done is thought about it and talked about it. A diagram gives your eye an opportunity to check out what your imagination has been up to.

Although your diagram does not have to look like a professional draftsman's, it should be drawn more or less to scale. This helps give you a feel for the proportions of the piece and also enables you to modify or finalize features of the design.

The drawing should also include all of the relevant dimensions of the piece. When figuring out the dimensions, remember to consider the *thickness* of the wood itself. Remarkably enough, this is something which is often overlooked.

Don't be ashamed to spend time on your diagram, and make sure it's exactly what you want before you go ahead with the actual work. It's considerably easier to make changes on your diagram than to make them on the wood once you've started working with it.

A practice that can sometimes be used in conjunction with your diagram (though not in place of it) is making a three-dimensional life-size model of your project. This has the obvious advantage of allowing you to see exactly the relative size and lines of your finished project directly in the space you intend for it. Such a model need not be elaborate; for example, you can use a sheet of cardboard and a box to give you an idea of the lines and bulk of a table you intend to build. The time spent on such a model often turns out to be very worthwhile in terms of catastrophes avoided, and it should be seriously considered if you are at all uncertain about your design or dimensions.

A sample diagram for a bookcase is illustrated in figure 14.

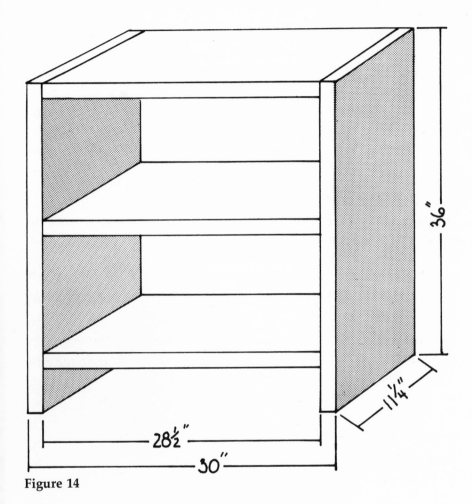

Figure 14

Materials List and Layout

The next step in your project is to determine the amount of wood you will need to complete it. To accomplish this, first take your diagram and make a list of all the pieces you are going to need, according to their dimensions. This is known in the trade as a *materials list*. The materials list for the bookcase in figure 14 would therefore be as follows:

2 lengths 1 × 12 #2 pine 36'' long
4 lengths 1 × 12 #2 pine 28-1/2'' long
1 section 1/4'' A-C plywood 36'' × 30''

If you intend to cut the wood yourself, you next have to establish what lengths you want from the lumberyard. By and large, you're better off choosing the *longest* lengths that your method of transporting allows for. There are a number of good reasons for this. First, longer lengths in all lumber tend to be of better quality than the shorter lengths, perhaps because of the way it's taken from the tree. Second, by cutting a number of pieces from a longer length, you reduce the number of end pieces that you have to deal with. The ends of boards are often split and checked and therefore unusable. Using longer boards thus reduces your waste. Third, shorter pieces available at lumberyards are often scraps, which may have been cut off because of their undesirability. Shorter pieces left standing also have a greater tendency to warp or bow. Fourth, longer pieces will permit you the flexibility of changing dimensions or correcting miscalculations once you've bought the wood.

Of course, the disadvantages of buying longer pieces consist in problems of transportation and storage. Therefore, it may be worth your while to have the lumberyard do your cutting, and also because its radial-arm or table saws will give you perfectly square cuts. And if you are on hand when the cutting is done, you can insure that no inferior pieces will be used.

When figuring out your materials list, you naturally don't want to buy a lot of excess lumber that you're not going to use. On the other hand, you do have to allow a certain excess for saw kerfs (a *kerf* is the thickness of the saw blade as it makes its cut, which is approximately 1/8''), split and checked ends, knots and blemishes in the wrong places, etc. Thus, if what you need is four 3'-long boards, don't order one 12'-long board, as it will not be sufficient.

Therefore, the pieces we would want to order for the bookcase in figure 14 might reasonably be as follows: one 7' length 1 × 12 #2 pine (to make two 36'' lengths) and one 10' length (to make four 28-1/2'' lengths).

Laying out plywood is a little more involved than planning for regular-dimension boards. The easiest way is to make a sketch of the size sheet you are going to buy (usually 4' × 8' or 4' × 4') and then divide it according to your requirements, numbering the individual pieces. For example, if we were making the entire bookcase in figure 14 out of 3/4'' A-C plywood, our layout would be as in figure 15.

While with A-C plywood there isn't the problem with splits, checks, and knots, it is necessary to leave enough excess for the width of the saw kerfs.

Another thing to keep in mind in plywood layout is the direction that the grain is running. When cutting rectangular-shaped pieces, it's usually preferable to have the grain running in the same direction as the longest dimension; the resulting piece is stronger, the longitudinal cut leaves an edge that is smoother and less ragged than the crosscut edge, and the piece looks more like a natural piece of solid lumber.

In addition, grains should run in the same direction on those pieces that form a visual line with one another.

Figure 15

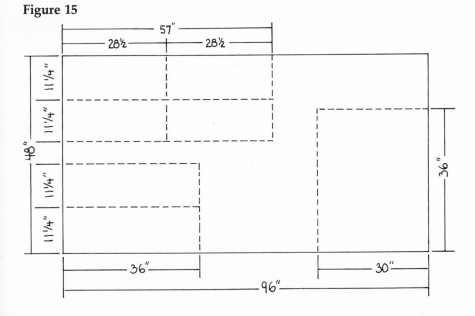

Measuring and Marking

Measuring

There is great wisdom in the old adage "Measure twice, cut once." It is an unpleasant feeling indeed to realize you've made a mistake in measurement after the cut has been made or, worse still, the project completed. As the keystone of all cabinetmaking, it is literally impossible to take too much care in securing accurate measurements.

The traditional devices for taking measurements are basically two—the *extension rule* and the *retractable metal tape* (figure 16*c, d*). Though the extension rule has the advantage of rigidity, I find it somewhat cumbersome to use. My preference is for the retractable tape; it's compact, easy to use, and quite accurate if used correctly. The hook on the end of most good tapes slides back and forth the length of its own thickness to enable you to take accurate outside or inside dimensions. In the case of all measurements, it is absolutely essential to make sure that the tape is held *taut* and is on a *straight line* between the two points that you are measuring.

When taking measurements of spaces such as ceiling heights or distances between walls, take measurements from a series of different points along the length in question. Virtually no floors, ceilings, and walls in any apartment or house are perfectly square to each other, and you will find that these measurements will vary.

Figure 16 Measurement devices. (a) Marking gauge. (b) Wing dividers. (c) Extension rule. (d) Retractable metal tape. (e) Metal ruler. (f) Combination square.

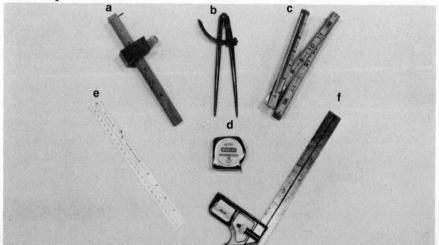

It's a good idea to keep in mind that whatever you build, it will never be any better than the accuracy of the measurements upon which it is based.

Marking

Laying out material and measurement require marking points and drawing lines on the wood. For straight lines, you need a rigid *straightedge*, like a metal ruler or yardstick. For marking points and drawing lines at 45- and 90-degree angles to the edges of the wood, a *combination square* is indispensable. It is also useful for short measurements and checking the squareness of corners, and it can also be used as a level (figure 16*f*).

Drawing curved lines is accomplished by using a *compass* or a set of *wing dividers* (figure 16*b*).

As far as marking implements are concerned, I prefer a *sharp pencil*. By marking the exact measurement, you can then put the saw kerf on the outside of the mark. Traditional carpenter's pencils have thick points, which are meant to represent the width of the saw kerf. However, I've found that this form of marking is not quite as accurate.

Cutting

Cutting lumber can be one of the more frustrating aspects of building furniture, depending upon the tools you use and your level of expertise. Any given lumber cut involves two planes, a horizontal and a vertical. For a cut to be successful, both these planes must be cut at the correct degree of angularity. When these planes are at an angle of 90 degrees to each other, we say that the cut is a *square cut* (figure 17).

Although most cuts made are square cuts, this is not always the case. In figure 18, we see exemplified a *miter cut*, a *bevel cut*, and a *double bevel cut*.

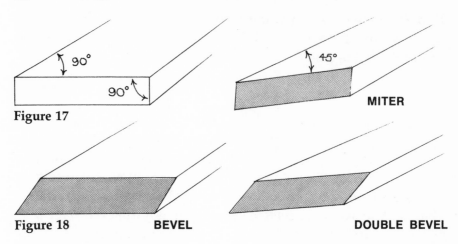

Figure 17

MITER

Figure 18   BEVEL   DOUBLE BEVEL

These different kinds of cuts can be effected by using a variety of cutting implements or saws.

Handsaw

The age-old method of cutting wood is with a *handsaw*, pictured in figure 19. There are three different types of handsaws with three different cutting actions: *ripsaws*, used for cutting with the grain; *crosscut saws*, used for cutting across the grain; and *combination saws*, used for cutting both with and across the grain.

Cutting accurately with a handsaw is a complex and fairly difficult procedure that requires concentration and practice. As we noted earlier, each cut has two angular dimensions or planes, and doing both accurately with a handsaw is a real challenge.

The proper position for using a handsaw is demonstrated in figure 20. Most of the cutting action takes place on the forward stroke when pressure is applied. The saw is then returned to the ready position on the backward stroke. Begin sawing with short strokes and gradually lengthen to long, smooth strokes. It is necessary to use your hand or knee or both to anchor the piece that you are cutting unless the wood is clamped to the bench or sawhorse.

One technique you may find helpful in getting accurate cuts is to clamp a straight piece of wood along the line to be cut. By keeping the sawblade flush against this guide, you are insuring that both aspects of the cut (vertical and horizontal) are correct (figure 20).

In all types of cutting, you will notice that the bottom edge of the cut splinters along the edge where the sawteeth exit, especially on crosscut. This can be avoided if you place a scrap piece of wood underneath the one you are cutting. Other somewhat less effective methods for avoiding this splintering include scoring the underside line of cut with a sharp blade or placing masking tape along this line. Because of this difficulty with splintering, always cut with the good side of the wood facing up.

Another difficulty in using a handsaw involves the end of the cut, when the unsupported half of the piece you are cutting has a tendency to fall before you have completed the cut, ripping off part of the supported board. This can be avoided by having yourself or someone else support the unsupported piece when you get near the end. Or you can rest both halves on supports and cut in between the supports. Using this

Figure 20

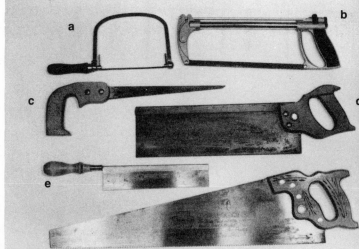

Figure 19 Saws. (a) Coping saw. (b) Hacksaw.
(c) Keyhole saw. (d) Backsaw. (e) Small backsaw.
(f) Combination handsaw.

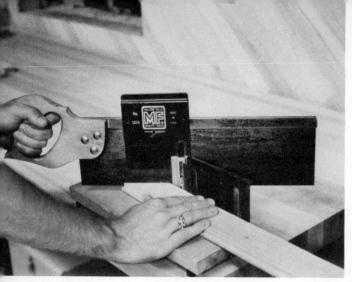
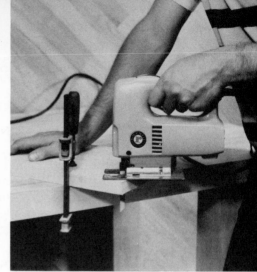

Figure 21   Figure 22

method, however, you will find that as you get near the end of the cut, the two pieces will gradually close together and bind the saw blade. This can be avoided by lifting the two pieces slightly to complete the cut or by placing a wedge like the blade of a screwdriver at the opening of the cut to keep the two halves apart.

Backsaw and Miter Box

A *backsaw* is a special kind of handsaw that has a stiff reinforced blade and small teeth set close together for fine cutting (figure 19*d; e*). Both of these features help in making more accurate (although much slower) cuts. The backsaw is normally used in conjunction with a *miter box*, a device for holding the saw and anchoring it in different positions as you cut (figure 21). The backsaw and miter box are not practical for large pieces of lumber, but they are extremely effective for smaller pieces such as trim and moldings, where extreme accuracy is required.

Saber Saw

The *saber saw*, pictured in figure 22, is an extremely versatile power tool. Utilizing a variety of interchangeable blades with a reciprocating (up-and-down) motion, it is chiefly used for its ability to cut curves, irregular shapes, and interior cuts. However, it is also quite effective for cutting straight lines, particularly when the metal edge guide provided with the tool is used, or when a piece of lumber is clamped alongside the line of cut to act as a guide. There are a variety of different blades available for it that enable you to make different kinds of cuts in different kinds of materials. In addition, the platform of the saw is adjustable, enabling you to make bevel cuts at the angle of your choosing. The saber saw is truly a jack of all trades, as well as being a master of some.

Because of the action of the blade—the teeth cut up through the wood—remember to cut with the good side of the material facing down to avoid splintering the good side.

Circular Saw

The *circular saw,* pictured in figure 23, is a power tool designed to help you make straight, accurate cuts with a minimum of effort. It is also a potentially lethal implement of human destruction, and extreme care should be exercised with it at all times.

The saw is made to insure accurate cuts on the vertical plane simply by keeping the saw platform flush against the work surface. The angle of the blade relative to this platform is adjustable, allowing you to make bevel cuts.

Accuracy on the horizontal plane is achieved either by a steady hand, a metal rip guide normally provided with the saw, or by clamping a block of wood parallel to the cut to act as a guide.

Figure 23

Figure 24   Figure 25

Circular saws come with a variety of different blades for different types of cutting (rip, crosscut, combination) and for different kinds of materials. Since the blade of the saw cuts up through the wood, your material should be placed with the good side facing down to minimize splintering on that side.

With respect to the problem of the unsupported piece of wood near the end of your cut, the same principles apply as with the use of the handsaw.

The circular saw can be a great boon to the woodworker, but it requires practice, and I again would caution you to be as careful as possible when using it. Read the manual thoroughly before using it and remember:

(1) always unplug the saw before changing blades;
(2) if possible, clamp the wood you are cutting so that both your hands can remain on the saw and off the surface you are cutting;
(3) do not overextend your reach when cutting with it, or you may lose control in case the blade kicks back or when the saw leaves the surface of the wood at the end of the cut.

Radial-Arm Saw

A *radial-arm saw*, pictured in figure 24, is in my mind the Rolls Royce of cutting implements. Although it is designed primarily for crosscuts, the blade can be revolved and locked 90 degrees in either direction for ripping lengthwise (figure 25). The carriage of the saw also adjusts and locks for accurate miter and bevel cuts.

When used properly, the radial-arm saw insures an accuracy that is simply unattainable with hand tools. Additionally, the design of the saw eliminates the problem of the unsupported piece of wood and mitigates the problem of splintering.

Many people are unsure whether to buy a radial-arm saw or its chief competitor, the *table saw*. I find the radial-arm saw preferable for a number of reasons. First, most of the cuts you make are crosscuts, which the radial-arm saw specializes in but which are somewhat awkward on the table saw (especially with longer pieces). Second, I feel that the radial-arm saw is much safer, because the blade moves while your hands remain stationary, just the opposite of the table saw. Third, the radial-arm saw takes dado attachments for cutting grooves (a technique we will examine later in this chapter), a feature which the table saw normally does not have. Although the table saw is excellent for ripping (especially sheets of plywood) and for bevel cuts, the radial-arm saw also adjusts for most cuts of this nature.

If you anticipate doing any amount of woodworking in your future, and if you have the space for it, a radial-arm saw is a very worthwhile investment.

Cutting Curves

Not all of the lines you may want to cut in lumber will be straight, and there are special saws for cutting curves.

In the handsaw variety, two such saws are the *keyhole saw* and the *coping saw*. The keyhole saw (figure 19c) is used for cutting gradual curves and for making cuts in the center of the material from a drilled hole. The coping saw (figure 19a) has a much thinner blade than the keyhole saw and is used for cutting sharper curves and intricate designs.

These two handsaws have their counterparts in power tools. The keyhole saw in the power-tool class is the saber saw, which, as we have already noted, is an extremely versatile machine. In addition to cutting straight lines and curves, it cuts out interior pieces in material. A larger version of the saber saw is the *band saw,* pictured in figure 26. Its blade is a continuous steel band revolving around two large wheels. It is excellent for cutting medium to broad curves, and especially for working with thick pieces of wood. It is also useful for straight cuts where a vertical blade is required.

The power *jigsaw,* or *scroll saw,* is used for the same basic purpose as the coping saw—tight curves and intricate patterns. It is easy to work with (although watch those fingers), and you can really let loose your creative impulses.

Lumberyard Cuts

As we have previously touched upon, many lumberyards will cut wood you order with their own table saws and radial-arm saws. Some yards charge per cut (e.g., $0.25/cut); others don't. Lumber is usually sold on the basis of the nearest foot in crosscuts in the case of boards (e.g., if 5'8" is the length you want, you pay for 6') and the nearest square foot in the case of plywood sheets (e.g., if you want a section 3'2" × 1'9", you pay for a 2' × 4' sheet, or 8 square feet).

It is often worthwhile to have a lumberyard do your cutting for you, particularly if you don't have the equipment to make accurate cuts. The cuts they make should be nearly 100 percent

Figure 26

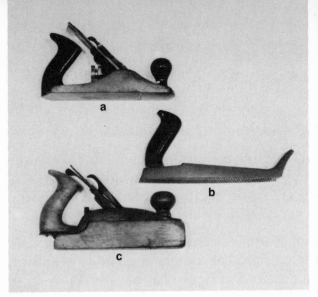

Figure 27 Planes. (a) Standard metal plane.
(b) Stanley surform plane. (c) Wooden block plane.   Figure 28

square by virtue of the tools they are using. One suggestion: Personally check the dimensions of your pieces before you leave, as mistakes in this area are not uncommon. There is nothing worse than getting home, all set to begin your project, only to discover that the lumberyard has cut all the boards an inch shorter than you specified! Not only do you have to cart it all back, but you also better have something in writing. Make sure, therefore, that your receipt specifies the cut dimensions you ordered. On top of this unfortunate incident, you certainly don't need an argument.

Lumberyards are reluctant to do any sort of exotic cutting above and beyond straight cuts, such as bevel cuts, curves, miter cuts, etc. If possible, be there when they do the cutting to insure the quality of the wood before they cut it. And, if you can, go to the yards during the week (Saturdays are usually hectic) and in plenty of time before closing. The quality of service varies greatly (as does the quality of lumber) from yard to yard, so don't be afraid to shop around.

Planing

Planing is a woodworking operation designed to accomplish one of two tasks: either "squaring up" or "beveling" the edge or edges when necessary. The *hand plane*, pictured in figure 27, is the traditional tool for accomplishing these operations. Always try to plane with the grain of the wood, keeping the plane steady and exerting a constant downward pressure. When planing across the grain, plane inwards from each end toward the center of the board in order to avoid splintering.

In the power class of planes, electric hand planers are available. In addition, the patriarch of the planing family is known as the *jointer*, and is pictured in figure 28.

Drilling

Drilling holes is essential for driving screws and inserting bolts. It is also necessary for many other wookworking operations, such as fastening hardware and hinges, hanging things and installing units, securing bolted butt joints, and making certain joints like the mortise and tenon. There are several different types of drills available.

In the hand-tool department, the best device for drilling holes up to 1/4'' (or so) is called an *eggbeater drill*, pictured in figure 29*d*. It uses special bits that come with the tool and that are normally stored in the handle when not in use. The drill is quite simple to operate, but it is a rather slow way to drill holes.

For drilling larger holes, the hand tool used is called a *brace*, shown in figure 29*e*. It uses special *auger bits* in different sizes for its operation, which are usually purchased separately. Special *adjustable bits* for it are also available that eliminate the need for stocking up on a lot of different sizes.

The power tool that does the job of both of these (except in special circumstances) is the *electric drill* (figure 29*a*). It uses both *twist bits* for smaller holes and *spade bits* for larger holes (figures 30*d; a*). The electric drill is quite reasonably priced ($10 to $35) and is an excellent investment because of the increased speed and accuracy it allows.

When drilling a hole, it often helps to use a *center punch* to mark excactly where you want the holes to be. Rotating bits have a tendency to move around, and this insures that the bit will be centered properly.

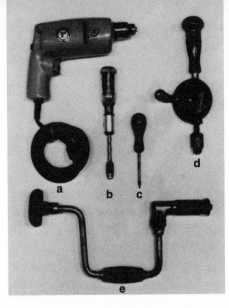

Figure 29 Drilling devices.
(a) Electric drill. (b) Yankee screwdriver. (c) Screw starter. (d) Eggbeater drill. (e) Brace.

To avoid having the wood splinter as the bit exits the piece of wood you are drilling into, there are two things you can do: The first is to use a piece of scrap wood as a backing, and the second is to complete the drilling of the hole from the other side once the bit has barely appeared through the surface.

There are occasions when you do not want to drill all the way through a piece of wood but instead just to a certain depth (e.g., when drilling holes for dowels or movable pegs). In those cases, use an *adjustable drill stop*, which fits onto twist bits and insures a uniform drilling depth. In the case of spade bits, I wrap a piece of masking tape around the bit at the required depth and keep a sharp eye on it. Devices are available that transform your electric drill into a *drill press*, permitting you to drill to any depth accurately and at a perfect 90-degree angle. A standard full-size drill press is shown in figure 31.

Figure 30 Drill attachments. (a) Spade bits.
(b) Stanley Screwmates. (c) Screwdriver attachment for electric drill. (d) Twist bits. (e) Masonry bits.

Figure 31

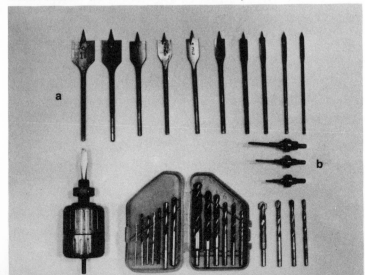

Drilling at a 90-degree angle without such a device requires practice and a steady hand. It is also helpful to sight right *over* the drill to make sure that you are keeping it square to the piece of wood you are drilling.

Types of Joints

The art of joinery is really the essence of furniture construction. Although there are a large number of traditonal woodworking joints, we will only be concerned with the most important and useful ones.

Butt Joints

The *butt joint*, illustrated in figure 32, is the simplest of all joints. It is formed by bringing the pieces together at right angles to each other. The construction of this joint requires only that the pieces to be joined are cut square. While it is one of the weakest joints, it is still useful in many instances. It is not a particularly aesthetic joint, as it results in the exposure of the end grain of one of the pieces joined.

Miter Joints

The *miter joint* refers to two pieces cut at angles (usually 45 degrees) that combine to form the angle of the joint (usually 90 degrees). As there are two planes of the wood that we have distinguished (vertical and horizontal), so are there two corresponding kinds of miter joints.

The *horizontal miter joint* (figure 33) is normally used for things like picture frames and cabinet doors, the *vertical miter joint* (figure 34) for those instances when an end grain is to be concealed along the edge of a joint.

The miter joint is an exceptionally weak joint and difficult to join, but it has the compensating factor of being aesthetically pleasing.

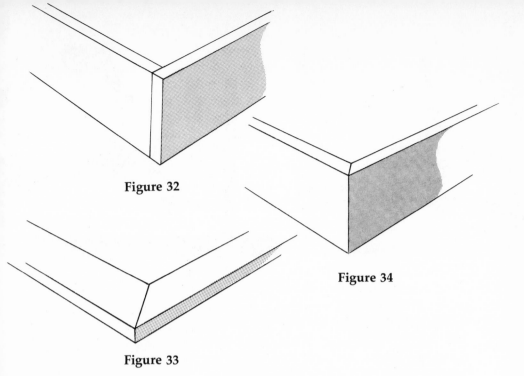

Figure 32

Figure 34

Figure 33

Dado Joints

Don't be misled by the fact that the *dado joint* sounds like a cartoon character; it's a fundamental joint that is indispensable for making much of the furniture included in this book and elsewhere. Illustrated in figure 35, it can best be thought of as a squared, rectangular groove in one of the pieces to be joined and into which the other piece fits snugly. This joint gives tremendous strength to a piece, particularly in the case of shelving or tabletops. When the groove is placed at the end of a board, the joint is known as a *rabbet joint* (figure 36).

Figure 35   **Figure 36**

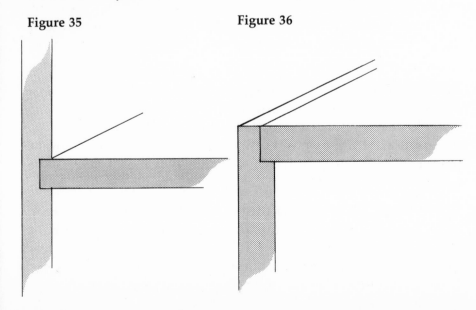

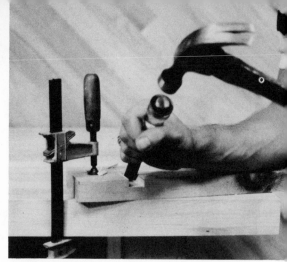

Figure 37   Figure 38

There are a variety of ways in which a dado groove can be created. The age-old method, practiced for centuries, involves using a saw, hammer, and chisel. This method is illustrated in figures 37-38. A typical selection of wood chisels is displayed in figure 39.

A second method for effecting grooves involves the use of a power tool known as a *router*. By using different-diameter cutting bits in a vertical chuck that rotates at high speeds, the router enables you to cut different-width grooves. It also adjusts to whatever depth needed for the groove. In order to insure a straight line, it is necessary to either use a guide provided with the router or clamp a block along the length of the cut to act as a guide (figure 40). With the large variety of different bits available, the router can also be used for doing decorative edge and inlay work and for trimming edges when working with Formica and other plastic laminates. By way of warning, the router is another power tool that requires extra caution in handling, particularly near the beginning and end of cuts. Hang on tight and keep your wits about you.

The third way of cutting dado grooves involves using the dado attachments for the radial-arm saw. Once the dado attachment is set to the proper thickness and the saw arm is adjusted to the proper depth of cut, cutting grooves becomes a simple matter of exercising your arm as you push the carriage back and forth.

Remember that the dado joint should fit fairly snugly. Another advantage of the dado joint is that it straightens out members that are bowed or warped. When fitting a piece into the grooves, tap the piece gently into place, using a piece of scrap wood as a buffer to prevent maiming the surface of the wood.

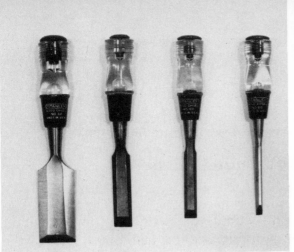

Figure 39

Figure 40

After a tap or two at one end, change to the other, and continue to alternate ends until the piece is in place.

Mortises

The *mortise* illustrated in figure 41 is used normally for insetting hinges to eliminate the space between doors and the frames they hang on. The easiest method for cutting mortises involves a *hammer* and *chisel*.

Mortise-and-Tenon Joints

The *mortise-and-tenon joint* pictured in figure 42, also known as the *tongue-and-groove joint*, gives tremendous strength to any joined members, no matter what size. This is why it was used almost exclusively for the main supporting members of Colonial barns and houses as well as furniture. It also has the advantage of being constructed in such a way that it can be easily disassembled. The simplest way of making a mortise-and-tenon joint is described in Project 21 (page 184).

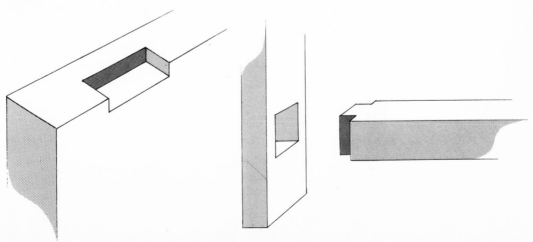

Figure 41

Figure 42

Fastening Joints

There are a number of methods for fastening joints together once they have been properly cut and fashioned. One of the oldest is the use of a hammer and nails.

Nailed Joints

There are a number of different types of hammers, as illustrated in figure 43. The most versatile one to own is a *16-ounce claw hammer*. The claw hammer also comes in the 20-ounce size and larger, but unless you plan to be driving a lot of large nails, as in building construction, the extra weight is actually a disadvantage. The claw of the hammer is used for removing nails.

Nails come in many different varieties. The two most basic types are *common nails* (with large flat heads or "hats" on them) and *finishing nails* (with small heads). These two types come in a graduated collection of different sizes designated by a number and the letter *d*, which stands for the word *penny*, originally referring to the cost of nails per hundred but now simply indicating a measure of their length. Thus, a 1-1/2'' nail with a large head is referred to as a 4d common nail, and a 3'' nail with a small head is termed a 10d finishing nail.

Figure 43 Hammers.
(a) Twenty-ounce claw hammer. (b) Sixteen-ounce claw hammer. (c) Ball peen hammer.

By and large, common nails are used in those instances when the head will be concealed after the job is finished. Common nails are thicker than finishing nails and, because of the large head, easier to drive. Finishing nails are used when the nail will be in an exposed position. The small head does not attract much attention and can be completely eliminated by the technique of *setting* the nail with a *nail set* below the surface of the wood and then filling the hole, as illustrated in figure 44.

Nail Size	Actual Length
2d	1''
3d	1-1/4''
4d	1-1/2''
5d	1-3/4''
6d	2''
7d	2-1/4''
8d	2-1/2''
9d	2-3/4''
10d	3''
12d	3-1/4''
16d	3-1/2''

If you are planning to drive a nail into hardwood or near the end of a piece of lumber, you run the risk of splitting the wood. This can be avoided by first drilling a *pilot hole*, a hole slightly smaller than the shank of the nail.

The nailed joint by itself is not a particularly strong joint. The only thing holding it together is the friction of the nail against the wood, and if the joint is subject to movement, or if it is under any real pressure, it will eventually loosen up. Exceptions are boxes, cabinets, and bookcases with nailed backs.

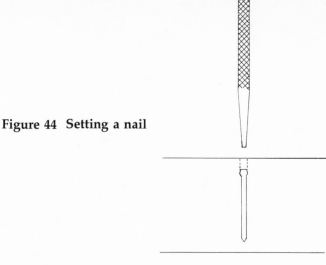

Figure 44 Setting a nail

Since the nails are driven at right angles to each other, they result in quite a strong unit.

When employing your hammer, use firm, steady strokes — no need to try to demolish the nail. When the nail is nearly driven, lighten up on your stroke so that you don't mar the surface of the wood with the head of your hammer.

Screwed Joints

A much stronger joint than the nailed joint can be had by using screws. As with nails, there are a variety of different types and sizes. The type used in virtually all wood joints is known as the *flathead wood screw*. Other types of wood screws, such as the *roundhead wood screw*, are available, but I have found few uses for these. Wood screws are threaded and tapered in standard proportions, and they come in various lengths and thicknesses. Unlike nails, different lengths and thicknesses can be combined, so two numbers are necessary to identify a particular size, the first referring to the length in inches, and the second referring to the thickness (ranging in consecutive order from 2 to 14). For example, a screw 1-1/4 inches long and a more or less standard thickness would be designated as a 1-1/4″ × 8 flathead wood screw. As the screws get longer, standard thicknesses get larger (for example, 3″ × 12 flathead wood screw), even though thinner sizes are available in these longer lengths.

As identified in figure 45, every wood screw has three different parts — a *head*, a *shank*, and a *thread*. To drive a screw properly, three different-size holes should be drilled to accom-

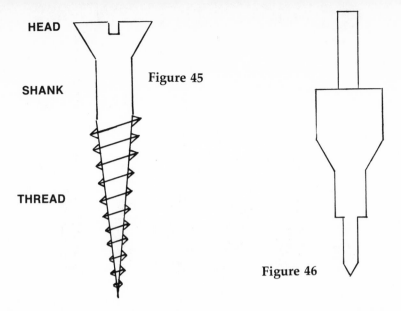

HEAD

SHANK

THREAD

Figure 45

Figure 46

modate each of these three parts. An alternative to using three separate drill bits is the *Stanley Screwmate,* which drills all three holes simultaneously and is adjustable for different-size screws, making it a tremendous time-saver (figures 46 and 30*b*). It also permits you the option of either *countersinking* the screw flush to the surface of the material (figure 47) or of *counterboring* it below the surface (figure 48). If a screw is counterbored, the hole can be filled with wood putty, a dowel, or wood plugs cut with a *plug cutter* from the same type of wood, thus concealing the screw entirely.

When drilling holes for the screws, leave the hole for the threads somewhat shallower than the actual length of the screw. This will give the screw more grabbing power, particu-

Figure 47

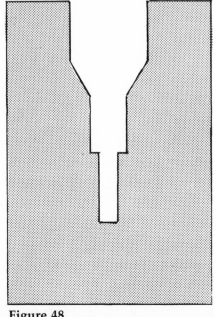

Figure 48

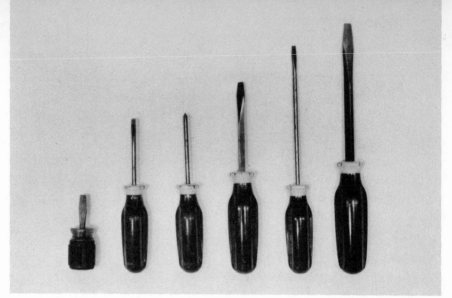

Figure 49

larly important in softwoods such as pine. Make sure that the hole for the shank is slightly larger in diameter than the shank itself. This will insure that the two pieces will be brought together tight as you tighten the screw. And if you lubricate the screw by rubbing it on a bar of moist soap, you'll find driving it considerably easier, especially when using hardwood or thick softwood. Screws are driven with *screw-drivers*, a selection of which is shown in figure 49. A power screwdriver attachment is illustrated in figure 30.

The screwed joint is far superior to the nailed joint. Not only is it many times stronger, but it also permits easy disassembling and reassembling. This is essential for modular designs and for eventual moving of large pieces. It is usually worth the extra time it takes to use screws instead of nails.

Bolted Joints

If a joint requires unusual strength and appearance permits, the use of bolts can be quite helpful. There are two basic categories of bolts that are relevant to wood joints: *nut-secured bolts* (including, among others, *machine bolts* and *carriage bolts*) and *lag bolts*. Both categories come in a variety of diameters and lengths and are designated by these two dimensions (for example, a 1/2'' × 4'' bolt would be 1/2'' in diameter and 4'' long).

The lag bolt is shaped something like a screw in that it has a point, but it does not have the screw's pronounced taper, and it comes with a square or hexagonal head (figure 50). It is intended to go through the first piece of wood and into the second piece and hold by the same principle as a screw. The advantage of it is that you can insert it using a *wrench* or socket set instead of a screwdriver; hence you can develop considerably more turning power (torque).

The machine bolt or the carriage bolt also comes with a square or hexagonal head, but it has a blunt tip and is intended to go *through* both pieces of material and then be fastened with a nut (figure 51).

For the lag bolt, a pilot hole is drilled somewhat *smaller* than the diameter of the bolt, depending upon the hardness of the wood. For the machine or carriage bolt, the hole drilled would be the same or slightly *larger* than the bolt diameter.

A variation of the simple butt joint with a bolt is shown in figure 52, which demonstrates how you can bolt two members at right angles to each other. This is a particularly good technique when using large, heavy pieces of wood.

Unless washers are used with a bolt, it is possible that the head or the nut or both may become submerged in the material as the bolt is tightened. If you plan to countersink or counterbore the head of the bolt, there doesn't have to be a washer under the head. Otherwise, you will need one washer on the lag bolt (under the head) and two on the machine bolt (one under the head and one inside the nut). The carriage bolt (figure 53), which has a self-anchoring head, needs only one washer (inside the nut).

Figure 50   Figure 51   Figure 52   Figure 53

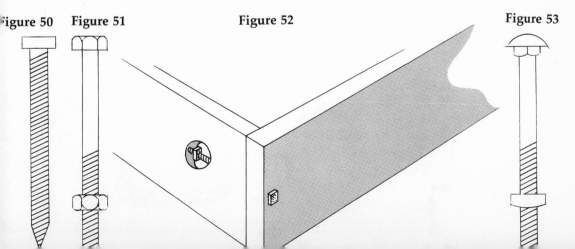

As already mentioned, the use of bolts is not always structurally or aesthetically appropriate, but when it is, they provide tremendous strength plus easy diassembly and reassembly.

Glued Joints

The glued joint, when properly done, can result in the strongest of all possible joints. The secret of successful gluing is to have the pieces of the joint fit snugly together and then to clamp the joint under extreme pressure until the glue has dried. The resulting joint is actually stronger than the fiber of the wood itself.

There are a number of different wood glues on the market. While a *white glue* (e.g., Elmer's, Sobo, etc.), is usually adequate, a *yellow glue* (e.g., Titebond) has over twice the strength.

There are several different types of clamps available (see figure 54), each appropriate for different kinds of joints. For a straight or perpendicular joint, the *bar clamp, pipe clamp* or *"C" clamp* (each is adjustable) are the best.

For a miter joint, a special *miter clamp* is made that locks the joint into place as pressure is applied.

For an irregular shape, the *web clamp* is the best to use. This type of clamp can be approximately duplicated with a length of rope and a straight object such as a hammer inserted between two of the strands of rope and wound tight.

Figure 54 Clamps. (a) Web clamp. (b) Handscrew. (c) Small "C" clamp. (d) Large "C" clamp. (e) Adjustable bar clamp. (f) Corner clamp. (g) Pipe clamp.

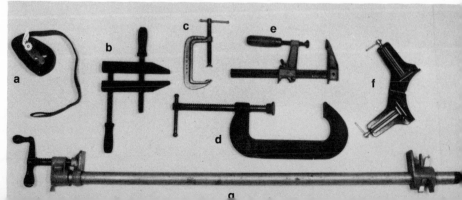

Gluing can be done in conjunction with the other means of fastening we have examined — nailing, screwing, bolting — and those auxiliary means can sometimes take the place of clamps (e.g., glue might be applied to the two pieces to be joined, which are then brought together and nailed, screwed, or bolted). For mitered corners, special corrugated fasteners are available that hold and strengthen a joint.

Using glue naturally means that the joints are not designed to be disassembled, so make sure that the joint it is used on is permanent. Gluing can also be somewhat messy, so have plenty of newspapers and paper towels on hand.

Installation

Installation of custom built-in furniture (bookshelves, wall units, lofts, cabinets) falls into two general categories — stabilizing freestanding units and hanging unsupported units. Both types of installation share certain problems, namely, the determination of *true level* and *plumb,* and the best means of attachment to the wall.

True Level and Plumb

True level refers to the same horizontal level that water achieves when left on its own (figure 55). True plumb refers to the vertical plane that is achieved when a suspended string or cord with a weighted object dangling from its end finally comes to rest (figure 56). True level and true plumb form a 90-degree angle with each other.

Figure 55

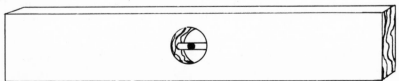

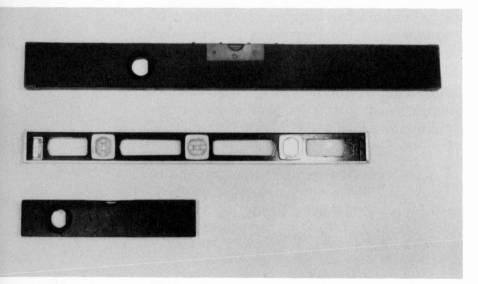

Figure 57   **Figure 56**

Since most houses and buildings are supposed to be perfectly level and plumb, you should be able (theoretically at least) to determine true level and plumb by taking equal measurements from the floors, walls, or ceilings. Unfortunately, due either to faulty craftsmanship or to the effects of time, most buildings do not have floors, ceilings, and walls that are level and plumb. Thus, you may find that a unit sitting flush on the floor looks crooked to the eye, or that a unit hanging parallel to the floor or ceiling, or square to the adjacent walls, looks askew.

The way to determine whether a unit is truly level and plumb is by the use of a *spirit level,* pictured in figure 57. This tool has two glass or plastic tubes at right angles to each other, one for determining true level and the other for determing true plumb. By centering the air bubble trapped in the fluid-filled ampule, you can determine what the true level or plumb really is.

Having read this, you should be forewarned that there are occasions when a unit may be truly level or plumb, but to the naked eye it may *look* crooked or askew relative to its setting. In these cases, you have to decide whether you want your unit to *look* level or *be* level.

Wall Attachment

To attach something to a wall successfully, you first have to determine what kind of wall you are working with. There are two basic types: solid plaster walls, often 3/4'' to 1-1/2'' thick over wooden lath strips or brick (figure 58), usually found in older buildings and houses; and hollow walls usually constructed of 1/2'' sheetrock on a wooden stud frame (figure 59).

If you are dealing with solid plaster or brick walls, the best means of attachment is accomplished by using *wall anchors*. These are variable-size jackets or tubes made of plastic or lead into which screws are driven. A hole the size of the anchor is drilled into the wall, the anchor is placed into the hole, and a screw slightly *larger* than the anchor's hole is driven into that,

Figure 58   **Figure 59**

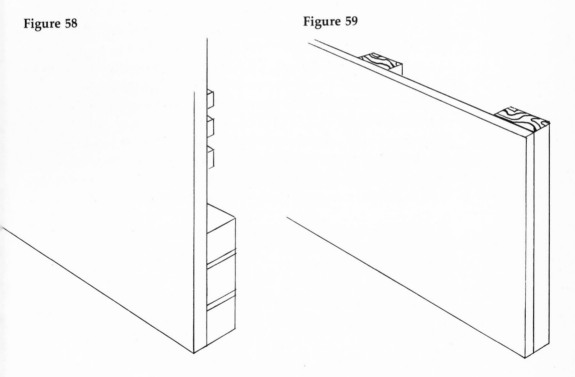

causing the anchor to expand and thus to be held in the wall by the pressure it exerts (figure 60). To attach a board or a bracket to the wall, the screw is placed *through* the board or bracket (in a hole slightly larger than its diameter) and then into the anchor, causing the board or bracket to be brought up snugly to the wall as the screw is driven home. The size of the anchor you use depends on how strong a grip on the wall you need — the greater the stress, the larger the anchor. As well as being sold individually, anchors also come in *blister packs* with instructions and the appropriate-size screws. Also, when drilling into plaster or masonary walls, try to use a carbide-tipped masonary bit, since a standard steel twist bit will dull very quickly if subjected to this sort of task.

There are two ways to approach hollow-wall attachment. The first is to locate the wooden studs forming the frame of the wall and nail or screw directly into them. The second is to resort to *hollow-wall hangers*. As far as the first method is concerned, the major difficulty is in locating the studs to begin with. But since the centers of studs are usually placed 16'' apart, once you've found the first stud, you've found them all. Sometimes studs can be located by knocking on the wall with a hard object (like your knuckles) and listening for a solid sound next to the hollow ones. Another way is to use a *stud finder*, many of which are available on the market. There are two types — one using a magnet to locate the nails in the studs (and hence the studs), and one using *Ford dowser balls*. As a final resort, you can drill a series of pilot holes until you strike wood.

Figure 60

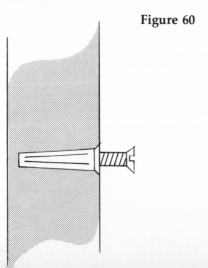

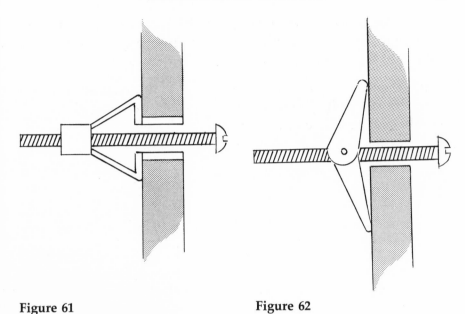

Figure 61   Figure 62

Often, studs are not located in convenient places for the purposes of your installation, and in these cases hollow-wall
hangers must be used. There are two basic kinds — *molly bolts*
for hanging smaller objects and *toggle bolts* for the larger ones.
They both work on a similar principle, as shown in figures 61
and 62. Boards and brackets are attached in the same manner
as with anchors, the screws or bolts being placed through
holes slightly larger than their diameter and then into the
wall to be fastened tight.

Stabilizing a freestanding unit is usually best done by attaching the unit to the wall in a few key areas, either through the
back (if it has one) or by using steel or brass corner brackets
(figure 63).

Hanging an unsupported unit is more complicated. If the unit
is small and light, it can be attached directly to the wall in the
ways we have indicated. If the unit is larger and heavier, it is
usually better to mount vertical wooden supports to the walls
(either 1 × 3's or 2 × 4's) and then attaching the unit to these

wooden supports. This method provides greater strength and is much easier than trying to attach the unit directly to the wall.

And remember, when mounting a unit to the wall, don't complete the job until you are certain it is aligned straight, level, plumb, or however you want it.

Figure 63

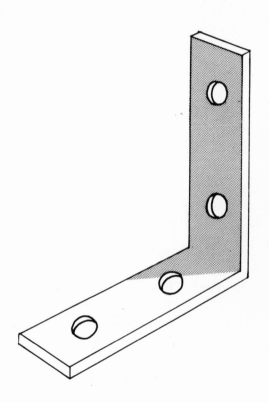

Wood Finishing

"Finishing is an art in itself, the study of a lifetime." I have heard this solemn pronouncement, or variations thereof, on occasions too numerous to count, usually (though not always) from the lips of those who have never ventured into the territory of wood finishing. I can't say that I really agree with statements such as these. Not that there aren't skills and knowledge to be mastered if one is to be a successful finisher, for certainly there are. However, I view finishing as simply another aspect of woodworking, neither more mysterious nor more difficult than other aspects. I think that woodworkers do tend to encourage this air of mystery about finishing, guarding their secrets with the tenacity of Colonel Sanders guarding his fried-chicken recipe. And when they do write books on finishing, you often find that you're more confused at the end than at the beginning, after they have wound you around their own idiosyncratic formulations.

All of this notwithstanding, I believe that the basic principles of finishing are relatively simple and easily grasped, and I shall endeavor in this chapter to demonstrate this.

To begin with, there are three distinct steps in finishing a piece of furniture, which always proceed in the same sequential order. The first step is the preparation of the surface, which consists in getting the surface smooth, clean, and free of foreign matter. The second step is the application of stain to the wood, to give it color, and to enhance its natural hues, grains, and textures. The third step is the application of the finish over the stain, for the purpose of protecting the wood as well as further enhancing its appearance.

We will consider each of these steps in detail in our effort to unlock the age-old mysteries of furniture finishing.

Surface Preparation

The primary task of preparing a wood surface for staining and finishing is that of sanding in order to achieve a smooth and clean surface. There are a number of different types and grades of sandpaper available, as well as a number of different ways to use the sandpaper. With all of these, the cardinal rule to remember is this: Always *sand with the grain* (whenever possible). It is the only way to achieve a truly smooth surface, since sanding across the grain invariably results in scratches, which then have to be removed by sanding with the grain.

Sandpapers

Sandpaper Types

There are several different types of sandpaper available. The two most common are flint and aluminum oxide.

Flint: Blond in color, this is the cheapest sandpaper available, and I would not recommend using it. It cuts slowly, dulls quickly, and clogs easily. In addition, pieces of the abrasive often become detached from the paper, threatening at a later date to groove and mar the surface if they are not removed. Although the initial cost is low, in the long run it's a case of being penny-wise and pound-foolish.

Aluminum oxide: Gray-black in color, this is the other type of sandpaper commonly available at most hardware stores and lumberyards. It is a tough and durable paper that cuts easily, lasts long, and resists clogging. It also comes in an *open coat* variety, on which the grit is not as densely applied, making it even more resistant to clogging, although somewhat slower in cutting.

Garnet: Reddish in color, this paper is not quite as tough as the aluminum oxide, although it too cuts very well and is substantially superior to flint paper.

Silicon carbide: Black in color, this is another extremely hard, abrasive paper that is used mainly for finishing metal and for very fine sanding of wood in the final steps of surface preparation and in between coats of finish. It often comes with a waterproof backing to permit wet sanding.

Sandpaper Grits

All sandpaper is graded according to the relative coarseness and size of the abrasive grit attached to the face of the paper. There are two common systems of grading sandpaper grits:

(1) In the *0 series*, numbers run consecutively from 1/0 (the coarsest) to 12/0 (the finest).

(2) In the *standard-grit*, or *grain-size series*, numbers run from 0 (the coarsest) to 600 (the finest).

Numbers from one of these two systems should be stamped on the back of every sheet of sandpaper. In addition to the numbers, sandpaper is also often stamped *coarse, medium, fine,* and *extra fine,* for the convenience of those unfamiliar with the system.

Sandpaper Backs

The paper backing of the sandpaper is also graded from A to E, the letters indicating the relative stiffness or flexibility of the paper; A is the most flexible and is found on most medium and fine grits, and D and E are the stiffest and are found on most coarse grits.

Most backs are matched up to grits in a standard fashion, and variances are only available on special order. Backs also come in waterproof materials, normally used in the final stages of sanding with very fine grits or in between coats of finish. With waterproofing you can sand using water or oil as a lubricant in these final stages, allowing you to achieve a smoother finish.

Sandpaper is also backed with various cloth backings for special-purpose use, such as sanding belts for power belt sanders.

Sanding Implements

The most basic sanding implement is your hand and the fingers on it. While this is all right for spot sanding and for irregular curves and surfaces, it is really unsatisfactory for larger and flat surfaces. In the first place, your fingers get tired rather quickly, and secondly, it's difficult to achieve a flat surface, since your fingers are not flat.

As a result, the best implement to use in conjunction with your hands is a *sanding block*. This can be purchased in a store, usually made out of metal, plastic, or wood, and it is available in different sizes. Or you can make one yourself out of a block of wood or whatever else is handy. In either case, your sanding block should meet the following requirements:

(1) The sandpaper should be backed with a resilient material, such as rubber or felt. The reason for this is to prevent the grooving and marking of the surface in case a piece of grit, dust, or other foreign matter gets lodged between the sanding block and the paper, or the paper and the surface of the wood. The "give" in the backing helps neutralize these irregularities that are bound to arise.

(2) The block should be as large as is comfortable for you to hold and to use on the surfaces in question. The larger the block, the easier it's going to be for you to get an evenly flat surface.

Since sanding by hand can be a laborious process, there are power sanders available to facilitate the process.

Disk Sander

The *disk sander* is available as a special tool and also as an attachment that fits onto a power drill. In either case, it is *totally inappropriate for wood finishing*. Not only is it difficult to keep level on the surface of the wood, but the rotary motion cuts across the grain leaving grooves that must be removed. You are really better off ignoring this development of modern technology for the purposes at hand.

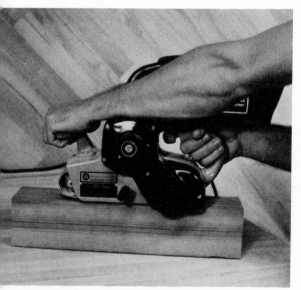
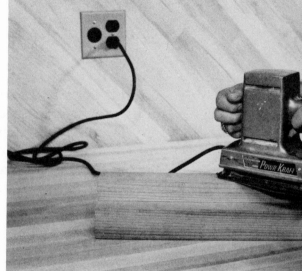

Figure 64   Figure 65

Belt Sander

The *belt sander*, pictured in figure 64, uses a continuous cloth belt that rotates in a straight line around two cylinders. Sanding with the grain, it is quite helpful for the quick removal of wood, or in the preliminary stages of sanding, when the wood surface is very rough. It requires some practice to use: It must be kept flat to the surface, for if it is tilted on its edge, it will quickly gouge the surface; and it must be kept in constant motion in a pattern of smooth arcs over the entire surface to insure a level result.

Orbital Sander

The *orbital sander* is the most common kind of power sander available, and it is quite excellent for medium and finishing sanding (figure 65). A standard-size sandpaper sheet is clipped to a felt pad on the bottom of the sander, and this pad then moves in a dual back-and-forth and figure-eight pattern at a very high speed (usually 10,000 to 12,000 rpm). As with the belt sander, it should be kept in constant motion to prevent an uneven surface. It is possible to achieve a very smooth surface using the orbital sander with very fine grit sandpaper.

In-Line Sander

For the ultimate in smooth finishes, it is necessary to use an *in-line sander*, which is similar in appearance to the orbital sander. But with this machine, the movement of the pad is strictly back and forth, allowing you to sand only with the grain. This is essential for total smoothness in the final stages of preparation and in between finish coats. Some combination orbital sanders are equipped with a switch that enables you to change from the combined orbital motion to the in-line motion alone and back again as necessary.

Sanding Procedures

Examine the surface to be sanded by eye or with a straightedge to detect high spots and depressions. Shade the high spots with chalk or the side of a pencil lead. Then examine the texture of the surface to determine the smoothest-grit sandpaper that will do the job. If the surface is already relatively smooth and level, there is no need to use a coarse-grit paper, which will only leave scratches. Sand with the grain, taking care to remove the high spots, and continue until the surface is level and evenly abraded by the grit you are using. Then move on to a finer grit and repeat the process. In the case of softwoods such as fir, pine, cedar, etc., you can save time and skip many of the intermediate grits. In the case of hardwoods, however, the more intermediate grits that you use, the quicker and easier you will get down to a smooth, even surface.

Between grit changes, it is essential that you thoroughly brush or wipe off the work surface to insure that no coarse grits remain to cause trouble when sanding with the finer grits.

While sanding, if the paper becomes glazed or loads up in any spots, it must either be cleaned (with paint thinner, turpentine, or alcohol) and dried or it must be discarded. Sanding with these spots will mar the surface of the wood.

Some woodworkers like to soften the backs of the sandpaper by moistening the smooth side of the paper with a damp sponge. The greater flexibility that results enables the coarse side to more closely conform to the surface of the wood, resulting in faster cutting and less clogging.

As you near the end of your preparation sanding (using fine-grit paper), one helpful technique is to sponge the surface of the wood with warm water (enough to get it thoroughly moist, but not enough to drench it), let it dry thoroughly, and then resume sanding with the same-grit paper you were using before the sponging. The sponging acts to raise the grain and wood fibers like whiskers standing up in shaving cream, waiting to be sanded smooth. If you don't sponge while sanding, the grain and wood fibers will be raised when the first coat of stain or finish is applied. Sponging also serves to level out the minor indentations in the wood surface by expanding the cells to a size comparable to the ones around them.

When you approach the final stages of preparation sanding and between finish coats, you may prefer to use sandpaper that has already been used and worn in. This worn paper has the advantage of a smooth and uniform surface, since the grits have already been worn down to a constant size and the sharp edges on the grits have been rounded. Using worn paper has the disadvantage of slower cutting, however.

As mentioned previously, the finer grits of sandpaper can be obtained with waterproof backing to enable you to apply lubricants such as water, light mineral oil, or raw linseed oil to the surface while you sand to produce a smoother finish. This technique is normally reserved for the sandings between finish coats, but can also be used in the final stages of sanding before the finish is applied.

The final step in surface preparation is to clean the surface thoroughly, using a brush, rag, and tack cloth. Once this has been accomplished, you're ready for the next step in the finishing process — staining.

Staining

As we noted in Chapter 2, different kinds of wood in their natural state tend to be very similar in color and hue. With the possible exception of woods like true mahogany, walnut, and rosewood, the colors we normally associate with wood names such as golden oak, cherry, and maple are the creations of man. Over a period of centuries, cabinetmakers and wood-workers have developed the distinctive colored stains that we have come to assume to be synonymous with the woods themselves. In actual fact, most of these woods can be colored quite successfully with most of the stains. For example, cherry can be stained walnut, and oak can be stained red mahogany. Some stains do look better on some woods than others, how-ever, and it pays to experiment on scrap pieces or parts that won't show before committing your piece to a particular stain. How you imagine a particular color is going to look is often not the same as the actual result, so take your time in making your choice.

Types of Stains

Stains are differentiated on the basis of the medium in which the dyes or pigments are suspended. Thus, there are *water stains*, where the dyes are dissolved in water; *alcohol stains*, where the dyes are dissolved in alcohol, and *oil stains*, where the dyes are dissolved in oils.

Water Stains

Water stains have the advantages of being cheap and easy to apply, and they are available in a broad range of colors and hues. In fact, since the dyes can be mixed to achieve different colors, the choice of hues is virtually limitless. Water stains are fairly transparent and as a result do not have quite the "body" and resultant richness of oil stains.

There are two main disadvantages to water stains. First, the application of water to the wood surface tends to raise the grain and wood fibers. However, this can be substantially reduced by presponging, and it is virtually eliminated by sanding between finish coats. Second, water stains are actually packages of dye that you mix with water for each use. Not only is this somewhat inconvenient, but care must be taken to achieve exactly the same proportions if you are mixing different batches for the same piece of furniture or trying to match a piece that has already been stained.

As already noted, water stains do not have the richness or body of oil stains, but this is not necessarily a disadvantage if you prefer a more or less transparent look.

Alcohol Stains

The main advantage of alcohol stains is that they are extremely fast drying. This can also be a disadvantage since it makes successful application somewhat more difficult to achieve.

Since they are not available in the same variety of colors and hues as water stains, there is little reason for the beginning woodworker to choose them over water stains.

Oil Stains

Oil stains are less transparent than water stains, giving a more substantial appearance to the color as it appears on the wood. Oil stains come premixed in cans, saving you from the inconvenience of mixing them yourself and insuring consistency from one can to another (although the very bottom of the can is often somewhat darker than the rest due to the settling of pigments, and it should be mixed with succeeding cans to insure consistency of color).

Oil stains do not come in nearly the variety that water stains do. In addition, they are difficult to mix to achieve different colors, they are more expensive, and clean up is somewhat more laborious. However, they do give a very nice result, and if you can locate a color or colors that you like, you may find that they are well worth using. We personally use oil stains almost exclusively.

Again, the key factor is experimentation, and the stains are normally available in very small containers as well as larger ones for this very purpose. Remember also that stains take differently to different kinds of wood, and it is therefore important to try them out on the *same* kind of wood they will eventually be applied to.

One word of caution: Beware of those stains known as *pigmented wiping stains*. Having ground pigments suspended in a medium (oil, water, alcohol, etc.), this "stain" is actually more like a paint. Instead of being absorbed into the wood and enhancing the natural beauty of the wood, they sit on the surface of the wood, masking and obscuring it instead of letting it be displayed in all of its natural splendor.

Stain Applicators

Stain can be applied either by brush or by rag. Although a brush makes a cleaner, quicker job of staining, particularly on large areas such as a floor, we prefer to use a rag on furniture. We find that it enables us to really work the stain into the pores of the wood, spread it evenly over the surface, and achieve an even, homogeneous coloring. However, a rag is awkward in corners and hard-to-reach places. A sensible compromise, therefore, is to use a brush to apply the stain all over and especially in the corners and crevices, and then to use a rag to work the stain into the surface, achieving an even distribution over the area.

Staining Techniques

The basic techniques for applying stain remain the same no matter what kind of stain you are using.

First, make sure the surface you are staining is clean and equally abraded. If dirt, grease, wax, glue, Plastic Wood, etc., is left on the surface, the stain either will not be absorbed at all or will not be absorbed equally in those spots, causing an uneven and mottled finish. Additionally, if the surface is not equally abraded—i.e., if it is smoother in some spots, rougher in others—you will also get an uneven appearance, since the stain will "take" differently in these different areas.

Second, plan your staining path in advance, dividing the piece up into a number of small, manageable single surfaces with such natural dividing lines as corners or separations in the wood. This is to prevent overlapping wet stain on areas where the stain has already started to dry, which would result in unsightly overlap marks.

Third, as an extension of this principle, develop your strokes in such a way that wet stain *never* overlaps areas where it has already started to dry. This sometimes means that once you have started staining, you will have to work quickly in order to avoid such overlap marks.

Fourth, always apply the stain in the same direction as the grain whenever possible. In those instances when this is not convenient, such as corners and edges, apply the stain across the grain and then lightly finish up by rubbing the surface in the direction of the grain.

Fifth, work the stain into the surface of the wood, particularly with open-grained woods like oak, to avoid missing any of the wood pores. Don't just make a single pass over an area with the stain; make several passes, using broad, sweeping strokes and actually rub the stain into the wood. Remember it's all right to overlap areas that have stain on them, provided that the stain has not yet started to dry (usually 30 seconds or so).

Sixth, if you are undecided about two shades or two colors, always stain with the lighter stain or color first. It is quite easy to make a surface darker by applying additional stain, but it's virtually impossible to make it lighter (the wood surface can be bleached, but this has undesirable side effects).

Finally, don't plan to do much, if any, touch-up sanding once the stain has been applied, as the surface will start to lighten in color almost immediately. If sanding is necessary, you're better off waiting until you have applied the first coat of finish, which will serve to seal and protect the stain on the surface of the wood.

Filling

In order to achieve a perfectly smooth, glass-type finish with open-grained woods like oak, it is necessary to use a *wood filler* before the finish is applied. In the case of close-grained woods like cherry or maple, a smooth surface can be attained without using fillers by putting a number of coats of finish on the wood surface, sanding between coats. In the case of open-grained woods, however, this technique would be extremely laborious. Of course, if you don't mind the wood's surface being some-what textured, though still smooth, using a filler is unnecessary.

The type of filler to use is a heavy-bodied paste with a silex base. In its natural state, it comes in a cream color, but other colors are available. Since the filler won't take stain, the color of the filler used should usually be darker than the stained color of the wood, so that it doesn't attract undue attention to itself. Also because the filler won't take stain, it is absolutely essential that the surface of the wood be stained *before* the filler is applied.

A thin coat of finish (such as shellac) can be applied before the filler is put on (check the can's instructions). This will protect the stained surface of the wood from interference by the filler and will also help you get a smooth, even surface with the filler.

Application of the filler is best achieved by first working it into the pores with a *stiff-bristled brush*, brushing additional filler across the grain of the wood to completely cover the wood's surface. When the surface of the filler starts to dull and no longer looks wet, scrape the excess off the surface with a putty knife or plastic playing card, or wipe it off with a piece of burlap, or use a combination of both techniques. Get the surface as clean as you can, as any excess filler remaining on the surface will interfere with the finish.

After the filler dries thoroughly, check for rough spots indicating excess filler on the surface. Sand these spots very carefully with a dampened piece of 600-grit waterproof sandpaper. Be careful not to cut into the surface of the wood.

Some woods with particularly large pores may require a second application of filler.

Finishing

Once the surface has been prepared and the stain applied and allowed to dry thoroughly, it's time to apply the finish, which will serve both to enhance the natural beauty of the wood and also to protect it. There are a number of finishes available, each of which has certain advantages and disadvantages.

Types of Finishes

Oil Finish

The *natural oil finish* is one of the oldest of the finishing techniques, and it is still applied today by many museums, antique dealers, and woodworkers. The original recipe called for a mixture of one-half linseed oil and one-half distilled turpentine heated to a temperature of 80 degrees Fahrenheit (away from the flame, since the mixture is flammable). The heated mixture is then applied liberally to the surface of the wood. After permitting it to thoroughly soak into the wood (usually a half hour or so), you can wipe off the excess oil. Then the surface is polished with a soft, dry, lint-free cloth. To build up a satisfactory finish, the original formula called for this process to be repeated once a day for a week, once a week for a year, and once a year for the rest of your life (or the life of the piece of furniture, whichever ends first).

Modern users of this original oil finish often dispense with heating the mixture and reduce substantially the number of applications. The result is still one that is hard, durable, and in a class by itself for hand-rubbed natural beauty.

Penetrating Resin Finish

The descendant of this original oil finish is the group of oil finishes known collectively as *penetrating resin finish*. Using different formulas and marketed under different names, these finishes are applied in the same manner as the natural oil finish: applied liberally, excess wiped off after a half hour, polished with a soft, dry cloth. The main difference is that a hard, durable finish is obtained after two or three applications, unlike the laborious repetition of the traditional oil finish.

Natural oil and penetrating resin finishes are distinct from other types of finishes in that they protect and bring to life the wood surface without forming a layer of finish *over* the wood, the so-called wood-under-glass effect. Instead, they are absorbed into the surface of the wood and remain an inseparable part of that surface.

Shellac

Shellac, a finish made from the exudation of the lac beetle, was the major fine-furniture finish up to the twentieth century, when modern varnishes and lacquers were developed.

Shellac has the advantages of being quick drying and having good adhesion and good durability. It also gives the wood a distinctive warm, rich coloring; it possesses an orange tint in its natural state.

Unfortunately, the main disadvantage of shellac is the fact that it is soluble in too many common liquids, and this has resulted in the virtual discontinuance of its use. Shellac is soluble in — and thus will have its finish marred by contact with — water, alcohol, ammonia, and strong detergents, rendering it rather impractical for furniture subject to everyday use.

Unlike oils and penetrating resin finishes, which are applied with rags, shellac — as well as lacquers and varnishes — is applied with natural-bristle brushes.

Lacquer

Modern *lacquer* finishes, developed in the early part of this century, have the properties of being the clearest, the thinnest, and the fastest drying of all finishes. Because of its speed in drying, lacquer is used very extensively in furniture manufacture, since numerous coats can be applied in the space of a few hours. The speed of drying also means that it is best applied in spray form, as it is very difficult to get a smooth, even surface using a brush. As with stains, butting up a wet edge against an edge already dry will result in overlap marks. And although lacquer provides a finish that is hard and durable, it is also rather inflexible and thus susceptible to cracking.

These considerations render lacquer somewhat inappropriate for use in the amateur workshop.

Varnish

Varnish, also developed at the beginning of this century, provides the hardest, most durable, and most resilient of all the standard finishes. Since it is resistant to water, alcohol, ammonia, detergents, as well as heat and hard wear, varnish is the most protective of all the finishes.

Originally made using natural resins as a base, modern varnishes are now using synthetic resins, the most popular being *polyurethane*. These modern synthetic varnishes are even tougher than the ones made using natural resins and, in addition, are easier to apply and faster drying.

Lengthy drying time has always been the main disadvantage with varnishes, since the extended time that the surface is still sticky permits dust, dirt, bugs, and other foreign objects to settle on it, making for a less than perfectly smooth finish. However, it is possible to achieve a very satisfactorily smooth finish if you (1) use faster-drying synthetic-based varnishes, (2) work in a room that can be kept clean and closed off while the finish is drying, (3) sand in between coats of finish, and (4) give a rubbing or waxing to the final coat (for a perfectly smooth finish).

Although traditional varnishes result in glossy surface finishes, many modern synthetic varnishes are also available in "satin" or "matte" finishes, to which ingredients have been added to tone down the gloss of the surface and give it a subdued, hand-rubbed look. These satin finishes are useful if you want such an appearance, but you do not wish to expend the time and effort required to rub the final coat with pumice or rottenstone (more later). The ingredients that dull the surface also reduce somewhat the clarity of the finish, so that not more than two coats should be used on any given finish. If more coats are desired, use gloss varnish for the initial coats, and then finish up with a coat or two of satin finish.

Varnishing Techniques

Varnish is normally applied with a brush. If you don't have one already, the first order of business is to secure a good-quality *natural-bristle brush* (nylon-bristle brushes are for use with water-base — latex — paints and finishes). With proper care, the brush should last you through many finishings. Purchasing a cheap, low-quality brush will only end up costing you, both in the quality of the finish and in the length of the brush's life. The size of your brush depends on the projects it is to be used for — not so small as to make the job tedious, nor so large that it is bulky and gets in the way. You may want to have several different-size brushes on hand for different-size jobs.

Begin by dipping your brush into the varnish so that between one third and one half of the bristles are covered. Retract the brush slowly from the varnish and lightly draw it across the edge of the can (or the strike wire if your can has one) in order to remove air bubbles and excess varnish. Start at one edge or corner of your piece and proceed with smooth strokes as rapidly as is comfortable. Start each new stroke on a dry surface and draw it toward the previous stroke, finishing by lightly floating up and over the previous stroke. This will help insure a smooth, even distribution of varnish where your brushstrokes meet. If a new stroke is started on a wet area, an excess of varnish will be deposited, and overlap marks will result if it is not smoothed out. Every few strokes, draw both sides of the brush across the can edge or strike wire to dry it, and then lightly draw the brush tip across the portion you have just completed in a smooth, continuous stroke, thus removing surface bubbles and helping to smooth the varnish. This is known as *tipping off*.

On large surfaces, there is the constant worry of an area "setting up," starting to dry before you have completed adjacent surfaces, thus causing overlap marks on those edges where the wet will be butting up against the partially dry. This can be combated in two ways: (1) Work as rapidly as possible, and (2) brush according to a predetermined orderly pattern.

Proper lighting is also essential for spotting defects and missed areas. Finishing should take place in a generally well-illuminated area with an additional light that can be moved so that it shines across the surface *facing* you. Move your head from side to side and back and forth, causing every area of the wet surface to fall under direct illumination.

If you find that you have missed a spot, or that there is an uneven place in an area that has already begun to set up, do *not* attempt to repair it; you will only make the situation worse. Wait until the surface has thoroughly dried, and then repair the damage, either by sanding down the uneven area or, in the case of a missed spot, building up the spot with varnish and sanding it down smooth after it has dried.

On most surfaces, you will wish to apply at least two finish coats, as are necessary for a smooth, level surface. The more coats that are applied, the greater the "depth" the finish will appear to have. Give the varnish at least 48 hours to dry before sanding and applying another coat (the longer the better, as varnish gets progressively harder during the first few days after its application). Many polyurethane varnishes instruct you to recoat within 4 hours in order to insure proper bonding between the coats. The reason for this is that varnish does not bond well to a hard glossy surface. Unfortunately, 4 hours do not permit the finish to dry hard enough to sand. As a result, air bubbles, dust, and dirt remain imbedded in the surface, causing an uneven finish to result. This can be avoided if you wait 48 hours or longer and then sand between coats. The sanding will cause the original surface to be sufficiently abraded to allow the two coats to bond properly. Make sure that the entire surface to be recoated is abraded; any glossy patches remaining will indicate if you missed any areas. Use 400- or 600-grit sandpaper (usually silicon carbide) in sanding, if possible with an in-line or orbital sander.

Final-Coat Treatment

When you have achieved a surface you are satisfied with, you have several options available in treating the final coat of varnish after it has dried. You don't want to sand it, as you have the previous coats, since the dull surface that would result would not be particularly pleasing to the eye. If the final coat is sufficiently smooth and the patina is to your liking, you can simply leave the finish as it is and enjoy it.

If the finish is going to get hard wear, such as in the case of tabletops, and you want to give it some added protection, you can apply a hard *carnuba paste wax* to the finish and buff it to the desired patina. Apply a thin coat of wax with a moist cloth (some people place a lump of wax inside a moist sock or rag to insure thin, even distribution), wait a half hour, and then buff until you achieve a uniform sheen. Buffing can be done by hand with a soft cloth, with a buffing pad attached to an orbital sander, or with a regular *rotary buffer* with a *lamb's wool bonnet*. (There are also attachments for electric drills.) The rotary buffer is the quickest way, but the other methods are all satisfactory. Apply two or three coats at the beginning and restorative coats every three or four months. (Clean the surface first before applying additional coats so that dirt, grit, food, etc., do not become embedded in the surface.)

An alternative for finishing the final coat is to rub it down with a very fine abrasive to remove any surface irregularities. The resulting surface can then be either waxed or left as it is. (Actually, waxing and buffing alone will tend to smooth out the surface, making the rubbing not really necessary.) There are two abrasive techniques that will do the job. First, you can use 600-grit waterproof sandpaper. Lubricants should be used with it: water for a satin finish, oil for a glossy finish. This technique is much easier though not quite as effective as the second technique, which uses the traditional abrasives *pumice* (grade FFF) or *rottenstone*. These are abrasives that come in the form of powder (pumice is available at many drugstores). Each is used in conjunction with either water (for satin finishes) or oil (for glossy finishes). Acceptable oils are light mineral oil, paraffin oil, or raw linseed oil. Cover the surface with the water or oil (whichever you are using), and then sprinkle the pumice or rottenstone evenly over the entire surface (a large salt shaker comes in handy here). Rub the surface with a clean felt rubbing pad in the direction of the grain until the surface is perfectly smooth and the patina is to your liking. Clean the surface thoroughly, and then you can either wax it or leave it as it is.

Part Two

The Projects

1 Spice Rack

This home for your spices (figure 66) combines the natural quality of wood with the modern technology of Plexiglas to the mutual benefit of both. The lines are simple, and with the spices in their Plexiglas containers, the entire package is a very nice visual experience. The design is such that it can be made with virtually any number of wooden tiers, depending on the number of spices that you use in your culinary activities.

Each wooden tier is constructed out of a block approximately the size of a 2 × 4 about 18″ long or whatever length you require. A channel is cut down the center approximately 1/2″ deep and 1-3/4″ wide. The exact width depends on the width of the spice containers that you will be using; they should have a clearance of 1/8″ (figure 67). The channel can be cut with either a hand saw and chisel, a router, or a radial arm saw with dado attachment.

The piece of wood at the top of the rack is made from 1 × 2 stock, and is the same length as one of the wooden tiers. Both this piece and the wooden tiers can be made of either softwood, such as pine or fir, or a hardwood, such as oak. If softwood is used, buy clear lumber, since knots are not particularly attractive on a piece as small as this, and they are murder if you have to cut your groove through them.

After the wooden tiers and top piece have been cut, sand, stain, and finish them before attaching them to the Plexiglas backs. The Plexiglas you use should be 1/4″ thick, and it can be clear or any color you desire. Most places that sell Plexiglas will cut it to your specifications. Plexiglas is not especially difficult to cut (although a little slippery for hand tools), but have them do it if you can.

Attach the Plexiglas back to the wooden tiers by using 2″ × 10 flathead wood screws countersunk into the Plexiglas and driven tight into the wood (figure 68). Remember to drive them at least 1/4″ below the bottom of the channel in the tier. If you have clamps available, you'll find that they assist greatly

Figure 66

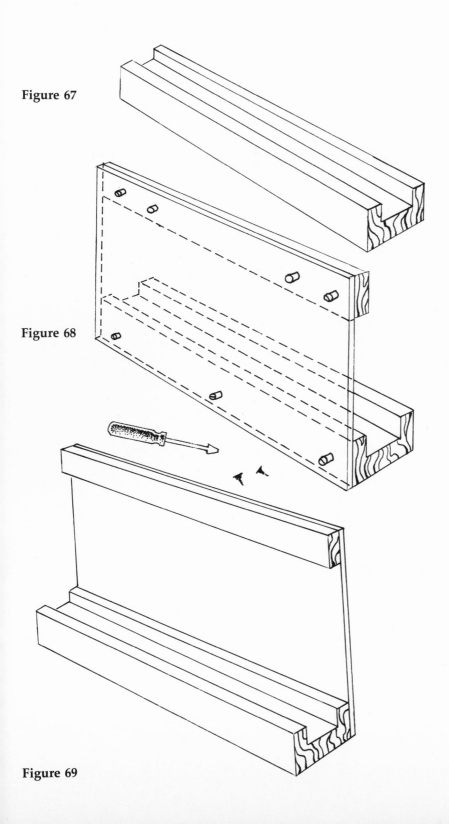

Figure 67

Figure 68

Figure 69

in holding the Plexiglas to the wood while you drill the pilot holes for the screws.

The top piece of wood is attached in the same manner, using 3/4'' × 8 flathead wood screws countersunk into the Plexiglas. After it is securely attached, drill two holes, one on either side 1/2'' from the top for hanging the rack on the wall (figure 68).

Plexiglas boxes in various sizes are normally available at the same supply house where you get your Plexiglas. Decide on the size box you want before starting on the project.

Extra tiers are attached in the same way as described above. Allow enough clearance between tiers to get the spice containers in and out.

Wooden dowels or something equivalent can be placed at each end of the channel to keep the spice containers from sliding out.

2 Wineglass and Goblet Holder

This particular little unit (figure 70) is ideal for storing wineglasses and goblets, and it minimizes the chances of breakage that you have with conventional storage. Popular in bars and restaurants due to its extreme functionality, it also presents a very interesting tableau for the eye, displaying much of your finest glasswear.

The basic piece of wood can be either a 2 × 4 (use clear pine or the equivalent) or a 1 × 4 (in a hardwood). The 1/2''-diameter holes to accommodate 1/2'' dowels should be at least 3/4'' deep, and care should be taken to drill them as perpendicular as possible, since any variance will be exaggerated by the dowels. Also drill the counterbored pilot hole for wall mounting at the same time as the dowel holes are drilled, since this is rather difficult to do once the dowels are in place (figure 71). Sand the block.

Figure 70

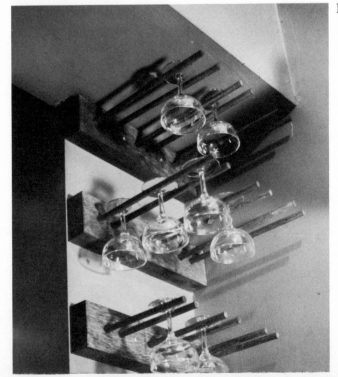

Figure 71

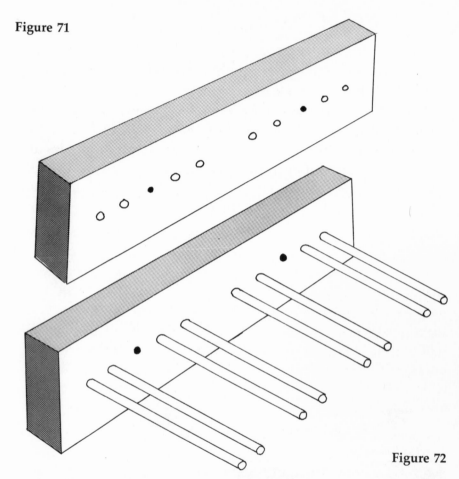

Figure 72

Make sure that the dowels you purchase are *hardwood* (usually birch), since softwood dowels will bend. Also make sure that they are relatively straight by sighting along their length from each end. Cut the dowels to the desired sizes, normally not much longer than 12''. If longer dowels are desired, move up to a thicker dowel—3/4'' or so. Once cut, tap them into the holes with a hammer (it should be a snug fit) after placing a few drops of glue in the hole (figure 72). Not much glue is necessary, and the dowel will force the excess out. If the dowels are slightly askew, try gently bending them into the proper positions before the glue has set.

Stain and finish after it has been assembled. Mount securely on the wall.

3 End Table I

These particular tables (figures 73 and 74) utilize an extremely versatile design. Either can be constructed using a variety of different materials and can be made to virtually any size. Each can thus function as an end table or as a coffee table, depending upon your requirements.

The sides of the table can be made of softwood (e.g., pine) or hardwood (oak is particularly nice). The most appropriate size lumber is about 1 × 4 for smaller tables, and about 1 × 5 for larger tables.

The legs of the table are simply 4 × 4's cut to the appropriate length, again depending on your specific needs. 4 × 4's are commonly available in cedar and fir. Cedar is an attractive wood with an interesting grain, a delightful aroma, and an inexpensive price tag. Its only liability is that it is fairly soft and will faithfully record the wear and tear it is subjected to. This vulnerability can be minimized if you use a number of coats (at least two) of a hard, durable finish (varnish or polyurethane) and show it a moderate amount of care and consideration.

It's been my experience that 4 × 4's made of fir (construction grade) are unsatisfactory for furniture, since they have never been completely dried and will tend to split and check as they do dry.

Those 4 × 4's made of hardwoods are of course the ideal — hard and durable, with beautiful grains and textures — but they are fairly expensive. Additionally, they are not stocked by most lumberyards; so you may have to do some hunting around to locate them.

The top of the table can be made of either wood, glass, or Plexiglas. If you decide on wood, your best bet is a lumber-core plywood with a hardwood veneer facing — oak, walnut, cherry, etc. Glass can be ordered to the necessary size and can be either clear or smoked. Check with your glazier regarding the proper thickness for the size of your top (usually 1/4'' to 3/8''

119

is sufficient). Plexiglas comes in many different colors, is quite strong, can be easily cut to size, and is quite inexpensive. However, it does show scratches and may tend to cloud up with time, problems you avoid by using glass.

Figure 73

Figure 74

Figure 75

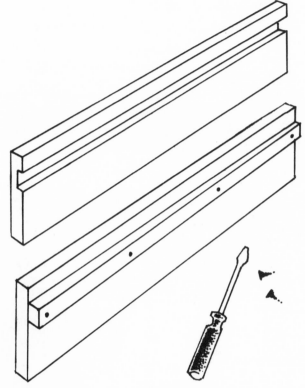

Figure 76

As far as construction and assembly are concerned, start with the sides. After having cut each to the appropriate dimensions, either cut a dado groove slightly larger than the thickness of the top you are using, into which the top will fit (figure 75), or attach a 1 × 1 wood strip (called a cleat) upon which the top will rest (figure 76). The grooves or cleats should be placed at a sufficient distance from the top edge of the sides so that once the top is installed, a ridge will be left around the edge of the table. Making dado grooves instead of attaching cleats involves a little more time, but it does result in a much neater and stronger finished unit.

If you already have the top in its finished dimensions before you cut the sides, make sure you leave a slight clearance in each direction (1/16″ or so) when figuring the dimensions for the sides. If possible, construct the sides first and then take the measurements for the top, deducting your clearances at that time.

After the grooves are cut or the cleats attached, assemble the sides with butt joints using 1-1/4'' × 8 flathead wood screws, counterboring and using wood putty, plugs, or dowels to cover the holes. If you have cut grooves, assemble three sides, slide the top in, and then attach the fourth side.

When the sides are assembled, attach the legs using 2'' × 10 flathead wood screws, counterbored, two on each corner to prevent wobbling. The tops of the legs should be positioned just under the grooves or cleats (figure 77). If the table is small enough, or the top thick enough, the cleats can be dispensed with; the top can rest directly on the tops of the 4 × 4's.

Following this, all that remains is for you to sand your table smooth, stain and finish to taste, and then sit back and enjoy your handiwork (figure 78).

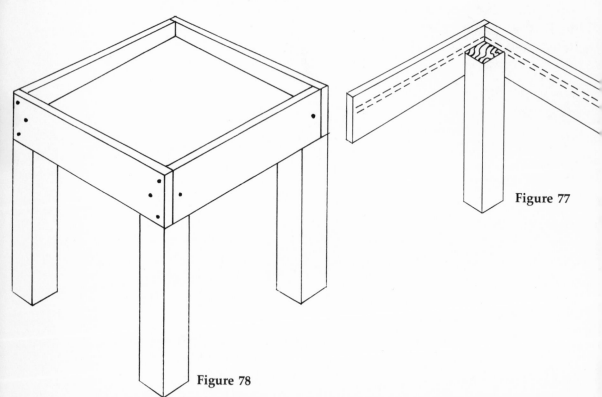

Figure 77

Figure 78

4 Bar/Counter and Bench

This bar/counter unit (figure 79) is quite simple to construct, but it is remarkably functional, and its clean lines and natural-wood quality make it extremely attractive. This particular unit was made using 2''-thick butcherblock for the frame and a sheet of oak veneer for the front panel. The contrast between the light close-grained maple of the butcherblock and the broad, sweeping grain of the red-oak veneer has a very nice effect. Other combinations of wood can of course be used.

If you want adjustable shelves under the counter, drill the appropriate 1/4''-deep holes for shelf holders into the butcherblocks that will be the unit's sides (figure 80). Either standard metal shelf holders or 1'' lengths of wooden dowels inserted into the holes can be used to hold the shelves.

The frame is put together using butt joints (although miter joints can be used if you so desire, provided you have the equipment to accurately cut the very hard maple of the butcherblock). The joints are held together using 5/16'' × 4'' lag bolts, counterbored and concealed with dowels or wood plugs (figure 80). Lag bolts are used here instead of screws because screws could not hold the joint securely and because lag bolts are much easier to drive into the extremely hard maple using a wrench (preferably a socket wrench) than screws are with a screwdriver. (The counterbored hole must be large enough to accommodate the socket or wrench.) Remember to use soap as a lubricant, and don't make the pilot holes too small, or you will never get the bolts in.

Either before or after the frame is assembled, attach with 1-1/4'' × 8 wood screws a 1 × 1 strip inside each piece of the frame approximately 2'' to 2-1/2'' from the front of the frame, to which the front veneer panel will be attached. In place of 1 × 1 strips, you could also use metal corner braces to attach the panel from the inside.

Figure 79

Figure 80

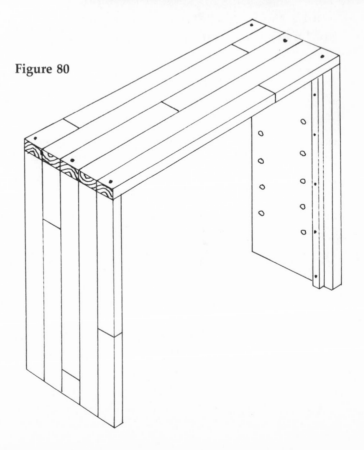

The unit can then be stained and finished. Butcherblock is usually left unstained and finished with a linseed or penetrating oil finish, though varnishes can also be used on it. A golden oak stain was used on the red-oak panel shown in figure 79.

Simple benches (figure 81) can also be made out of butcherblock in the same way the frame for the counter is constructed. In both cases, try to have the sides and top cut from the same piece of butcherblock (or other wood) so that the laminations, grain, and coloring will match up. It is well worth the extra effort.

Figure 81

5 Platform Bed

A platform bed (figure 82) is in many ways an ideal piece of furniture. Its lines are simple and economical, enabling it to be at home with many kinds of furniture styles and decors. The bulkiness of most beds is avoided by its low profile and the "floating" effect of its design. It frees the space above it and opens up the room. It is easy to construct and can be disassembled and moved without difficulty. The cost is quite reasonable, even if fine hardwoods are used. And the benefits to your back and overall sleeping well-being derived by substituting a sheet of plywood for your box spring are remarkable. In fact, you can finish the job off by substituting a custom-cut 4'' to 6'' piece of foam (it comes covered) for your old innerspring, and sleep the sleep of the innocent.

The construction of the base is the first order of business. The base, as shown in figure 83, is constructed using butt joints and fastened with flathead wood screws (2-1/2'' × 12 for 2'' lumber; 1-3/4'' × 8 for 1'' lumber), which are counterbored

Figure 82

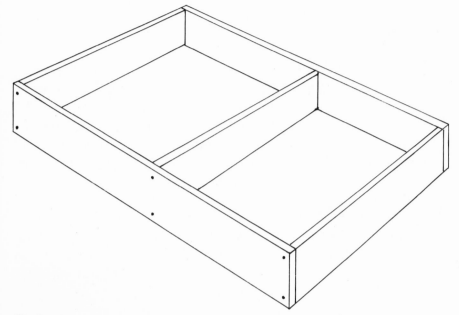

Figure 83

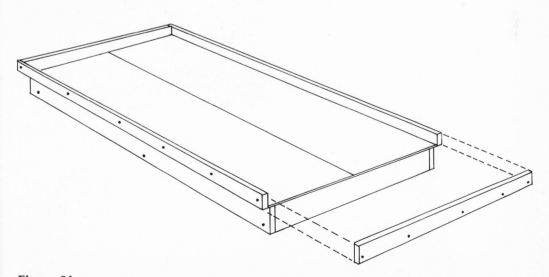

Figure 84

and concealed. The lumber best suited for the base is 2 × 10 or 2 × 12 fir or spruce (construction-grade softwood) or 1 × 10 or 1 × 12 hardwood, such as oak or birch (the former pictured here). Softwood, such as pine, only 1'' thick is not really strong enough for the base. One center support member should be sufficient if 3/4'' plywood is used for the platform.

As noted, the platform consists of one or two sheets of 3/4'' plywood that overlap the base 4'' to 6'' and are attached to the base with 1-1/4'' × 8 flathead wood screws, countersunk (figure 84).

The border around the edge of the bed, which serves the purpose of keeping the mattress in place, is constructed of 1 × 3's that match the base in type (pine for softwood; oak, etc., for hardwood). These boards are attached to the edges of the plywood using 1-1/4'' × 8 flathead wood screws, counterbored and concealed.

The bed pictured on the back cover has an apron of matching wood laid as a border around the mattress, serving a very useful purpose as well as enhancing the design. It has mitered corners and is attached to the platform with 1-1/4'' × 8 flathead wood screws, counterbored and concealed.

The exact dimensions of your bed—the height of the base, the amount of platform overlap, the size of the platform—will be determined by your own needs and preferences. Once construction is accomplished, stain and finish to your liking. The beds pictured in this book were stained golden oak and were finished with two coats of satin-finish polyurethane.

6 End Table II

This end table (figure 85) was originally designed to complement the platform bed described in Project 5 (page 126), but it stands quite well alone also. Its design permits the maximum use of the space both on the top and on the shelf beneath. Its construction details are such that it can be made in virtually any size and with almost any kind of wood.

The table pictured here was constructed using 1 × 4 solid oak for the legs, and 1 × 12 solid oak for the top and the shelf. Virtually any sturdy hardwood in a 1″ or larger dimension would be appropriate for both the legs and the top. In softwood, 1″ should also be adequate for the legs, though you could just as easily choose 5/4 × 4's or 2 × 4's, depending upon the appearance you wish to achieve.

There are two choices for the top and the shelf: Either they can be made from single sheets of veneer plywood, or they can be constructed by attaching together two or more pieces of solid

Figure 85

lumber (since standard solid planks rarely come wider than 1 × 12 size). Some lumberyards carry #2 pine in sizes 1 × 16, 1 × 18, and 1 × 24 (narrower boards having already been glued and sanded to achieve these larger widths). Using veneer is certainly easier than gluing solid boards, although you do have the edges to contend with, as well as the eventual possibility of chipping or marring the surface.

For those who want to stick with solid woods, the boards can be attached together either by gluing or by attaching wooden cleats to the undersides with 1-1/4″ × 8 wood screws, or both (figure 86). In both cases, use at least two clamps (depending on table size) when joining the boards and make sure the top surfaces are as even as possible along the joint. After the pieces have been firmly joined, sand them even along the joint, using a belt sander if the boards are substantially uneven.

Select the top and shelf before cutting the dado grooves in the legs, to make sure that they fit. We usually position the

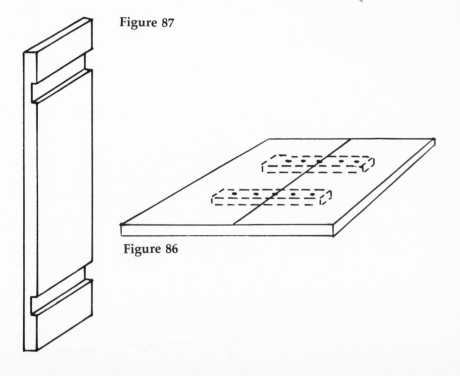

Figure 87

Figure 86

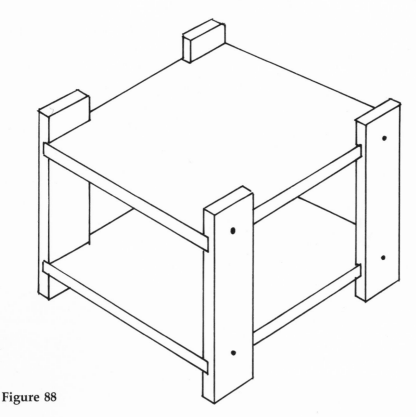

Figure 88

grooves about 1'' from either end (figure 87), but this is purely a matter of taste. Once the grooves have been cut, join the legs to the top and shelf either by gluing or by countersinking 1-1/4'' × 8 flathead wood screws (appropriately longer if legs are thicker than the suggested 1 × 4's), covering the heads of the screws with dowels, plugs, or putty (figure 88).

Stain and finish to your taste, but remember to apply the same number of finish coats to the undersides of the top and shelf as you do to the topsides. Unequal absorbtion of water by the pores of the wood is what causes warpage, and providing equal coats of finish to each surface prevents this. If you didn't use cleats, staining and finishing the undersides of the top and shelf also give you an unexpected side benefit of this design: It permits you to flip the table upside down, giving you a second table identical to the original!

7 Audio Units

This is a functional and stylish set of units for your stereo components, records, and speakers (figure 89). This system has the enviable advantage of easy mobility, particularly helpful when new furnishings enter your living space or on those occasions when you feel it's time for a rearrangement.

The component/record unit consists of four 1 × 4 hardwood boards (in this case, oak) with dado grooves cut in at the appropriate levels for the shelves (5/4 × 4 or 2 × 4 softwood can also be used). Each shelf is composed of either two solid planks attached together (see Project 6, page 129) or a solid piece of veneer-faced plywood. Fitted into the grooves, the shelves are then secured to the sides with 1-1/4'' × 8 flathead wood screws (appropriately longer if legs are thicker than the suggested 1 × 4's), counterbored and covered with putty, dowels, or plugs (figure 90).

The exact dimensions of the unit are determined by the size of your components—remember to leave an inch or two of "breathing room" above your amplifier to prevent overheating. Record shelves are usually about 13-1/4'' high.

Each speaker shelf is comprised of two solid planks of wood attached at right angles to each other with 1-1/4'' × 8 flathead wood screws, driven from the top piece into the wall piece and countersunk. Due to the weight of the speakers, two 1 × 4 braces of solid wood are also in order for each shelf. These can be notched to accommodate the two pieces, or simply screwed onto the sides of the planks. An easy way to get the proper angle for these braces is to lay one 1 × 4 across the edges of the two already assembled planks (which you are certain are perpendicular to each other) at the desired angle; then using the edges as a guide, mark the saw lines with a pencil, thus insuring that the brace will be flush mounted. After the first brace is cut, use it as a template for all others. Attach the braces to the shelves with 1-1/4'' × 8 flathead wood screws, counterbored and covered with putty, dowels, or plugs (figure 91).

Figure 89

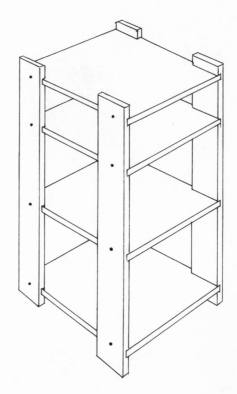

Figure 90

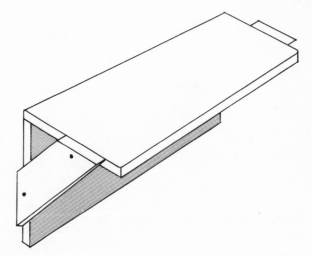

Figure 91

Stain and finish to your liking (in this case golden oak stain was used) and then mount *securely* onto the wall (speakers are heavy, and a fall can severely damage them).

8 Loft Bed/Bunk Beds

This is a uniquely versatile design for both bunk beds (figure 92) or a loft bed (figure 93). The bed frames are really independent modular components that can be added to or subtracted from the unit, and they can be adjusted to any height desired. This flexibility of design will be really appreciated as your living space, family size, and other factors change over the years.

The bed frame consists of four boards butted at the corners and fastened with 1-1/4'' × 8 flathead wood screws for 1'' hardwood or 2-1/2'' × 12 flathead wood screws for 2'' softwood (counterbored and concealed with putty, plugs, or dowels). Lumber sizes most appropriate are 1 × 8 in hardwood or 2 × 8 in softwood. The center and two end interior cross supports are either 1 × 6 hardwood or 2 × 6 softwood. Even if you use hardwood for the exterior frame, you may want to use 2'' softwood for these supports, since softwood (e.g., fir or spruce—construction grade) is considerably easier to work with.

Figure 92

135

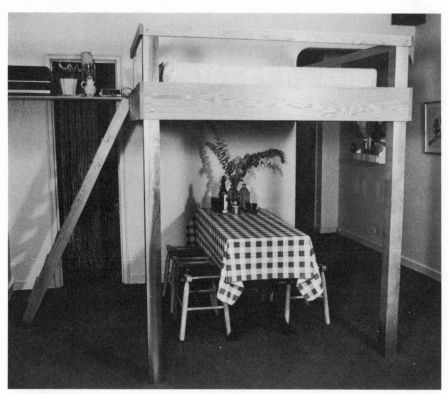

Figure 93

The dimensions of the frame depend upon the mattress size it will accommodate. The interior dimensions of the frame should be at least 1'' larger in each direction than the mattress, allowing you space for the sheets, blankets, and fingers that make the bed. Remember to add an additional 7'' to the length (or width) to compensate for the thickness of the 4 × 4 posts (3-1/2''). The mattress will not go around them unless it is cut to; it must fit either inside their width or inside their length.

Both the center and end supports should be flush with the bottom of the basic frame—this leaves a distance of 1-3/4'' between the top of these supports and the top of the frame. The reason for this is to create a recessed space that will contain the sheet of plywood and mattress and keep them from sliding around. You should leave a clearance of 3-5/8'' from the end supports to the frame corners to allow for the snug placement of the 4 × 4 posts against these corners (figure 94).

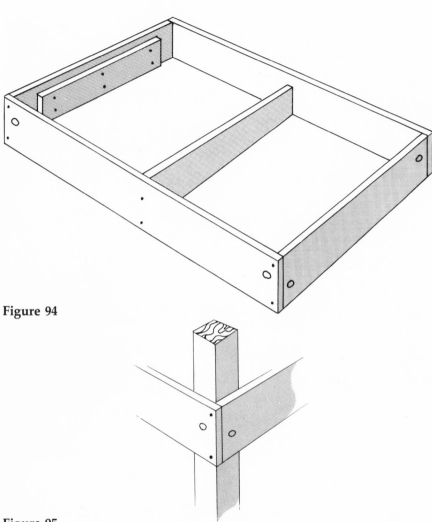

Figure 94

Figure 95

Once the frame (or frames) has been completed, it is time to attach it to the posts. These posts can be either a softwood such as cedar (pictured here) or a hardwood. Mark on the posts where you want the frame. Place the frame on its side (space permitting) and attach two of the 4 × 4's into place using 5/16''- or 3/8''-diameter carriage bolts. Use two bolts for each leg running at right angles (but not at the same height!), and tighten using nuts and washers (figure 95). The holes you drill for the bolts should be the same diameter as the bolts; larger holes would result in a looser joint. As the bolt and hole will be a snug fit, use a hammer to gently tap the bolts into place. Clean off any wood caught in the exposed threads of the bolt before putting the washer and nut on. Clamps are quite useful for holding the legs in position as you drill the holes and attach the bolts. Repeat with other frame if used.

Once these legs are firmly attached, carefully rotate the frame (or frames) 180 degrees to the opposite side and attach the remaining two legs in the same manner. Once these are attached, you can stand the bed into its proper position (figure 96). When moving the bed around, before and after it is assembled, always try to have someone give you a hand to prevent putting unnatural and excessive strain on any of the joints.

Figure 96

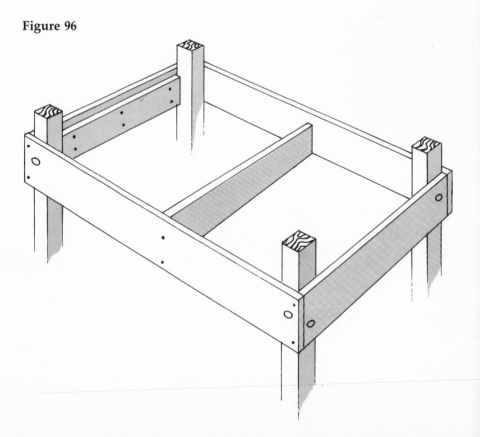

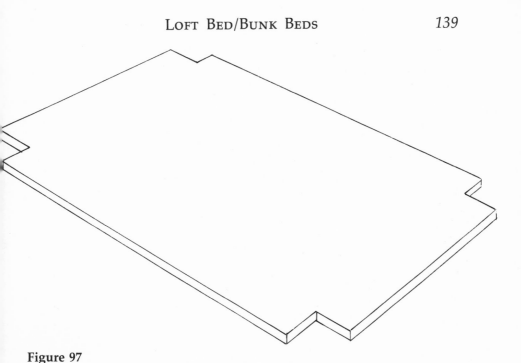

Figure 97

Once the bed is standing in place, you can cut the plywood sheet(s) to the interior size of the frame, leaving square notches for the posts (figure 97) and 1/8'' to 1/4'' all around for clearance. The plywood used is normally 3/4'' A-C. Set the sheet into the frame, and attach to the cross supports in a number of places with screws (1-1/4'' × 8) or nails (4d common). This will serve to rigidify the entire frame.

Since the space along the edge of the frame between the 4 × 4's (either the length or width, depending on how you choose to set your mattress) will not be covered by the mattress, you can attach 1 × 4 pieces of wood of the same type as the frame (figure 98). These borders can be used quite well for setting glasses, clocks, or food on.

In the case of loft beds, the bed should be anchored to the wall in at least one and preferably two places to stabilize the unit. Since the bunk beds have support at both ends of the posts, this added stability is not necessary.

If you are worried about someone rolling off the loft or top bunk, it's a simple matter to attach a safety railing to the frame of the bed to help prevent this sort of catastrophe. (Although the body has a natural reluctance to rolling off the side, even while asleep, it has been known to happen.)

Stain and finish the unit to your taste. As shown in the photograph, the posts for the bunk beds were stained a color contrasting to that of the frame, providing an interesting effect. In the case of the loft bed, both the posts and frame were left natural (unstained) and then finished.

All that remains is how to get up to or down from the loft or top bunk. This problem is addressed in the next project— building a ladder.

Figure 98

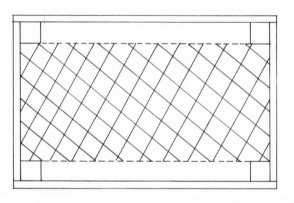

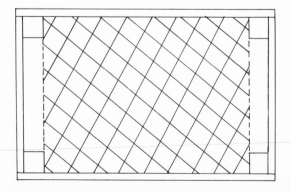

9 Ladder/Stairway

The ladder design pictured in figure 99 can be used both as a ladder for lofts or top bunks and as a stairway for any other elevation you need access to. The advantages of using this design for lofts and bunks instead of a simple upright ladder design are twofold: First, it is much easier to get up and down; and second, it is much safer. Of course, if space does not allow you to place the ladder on a slant, the ladder can be made completely vertical using the same joints and techniques.

The strength of the ladder lies in the dado joints into which the treads fit (figure 100). They give the overall unit tremendous strength, eliminate wobbling, and insure that the treads will never give way when someone is on them.

The lumber for the ladder can be either 2 × 4 or 2 × 6 softwood, or a 1 × 4 or 1 × 6 hardwood. The easiest method we have found for laying out the ladder sides is to take one of the boards and lay it up against the surface it is going to lean against. It's necessary to allow an extra 2″ to 3″ in height, which the ladder will need when the bottom corner resting on the floor is cut off.

Using a level, draw in the horizontal line for the bottom of the ladder, which will be cut parallel to the floor (figure 101). You can then measure up the board to get the corresponding lines for the stair-tread dadoes. Steps should be 8″ to 10″ in height. Also mark the vertical line at the top of the ladder side parallel to the surface it will be leaning against. Take the piece down and cut along the lines you have marked at the bottom and top of the ladder. Then cut out the dadoes for the treads, about 1/2″ deep for 2″ lumber, 3/8″ deep for 1″ hardwood. Using the completed side as a pattern, mark the cutting and dado lines on the matching side. Remember that the dadoes face each other, and hence they will be cut in opposite directions.

Use a hammer and a scrap piece of wood to tap the treads in place. Then secure them to the ladder sides with 2″ × 10 flat-

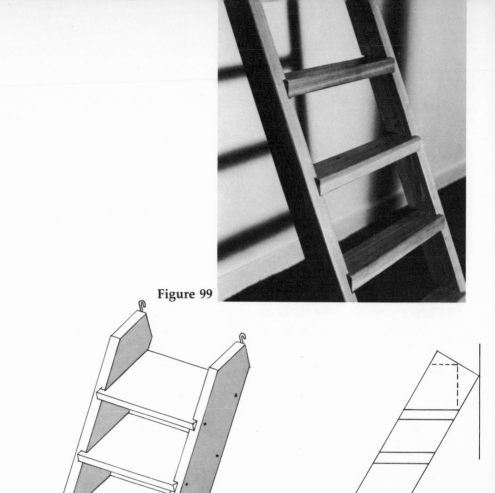

Figure 99

Figure 100

Figure 101

7-9"
BETWEEN
TREADS

head wood screws (for 2'' lumber; use 1-1/2'' × 8 screws for 1'' hardwood); counterbore and cover.

The ladder can then be permanently attached to the surface against which it is leaning, or large sparhooks on the ladder and matching eyebolts on the surface can be used to make the ladder stable but movable.

Stain and finish the ladder, giving the treads an extra coat of finish in anticipation of the hard use they are going to receive.

10 Bar/Kitchen Unit

This modular bar unit consists of three independent pieces that can be used individually or in any number of combinations. The three pieces are a cabinet for storing glasses and dishes, a unit for storing stemware with a shelf above for miscellaneous items, and a rack for storing wine and whiskey bottles. As arranged in figure 102, the three pieces form a nicely balanced whole, with the linear shape and volume of the cabinet being duplicated by the lines of the wine rack on the other end.

Construction of the cabinet, if deeper than 12'', entails using veneer for the frame, back, and shelves, unless laminated solid pieces are used. In this case, 3/4'' oak veneer was used for the sides, back, and shelves, while solid oak pieces were used for the doors, of particular importance due to the use they receive.

Before the frame is assembled, two parallel lines of 1/4''-diameter holes are drilled into the insides of the side pieces either 1'' or 2'' apart for adjustable shelves.

The frame was assembled using butt joints (figure 103), although rabbet joints would be equally acceptable. It is held together with 1-1/4'' × 8 flathead wood screws (counterbored and concealed with either putty, plugs, or dowels).

Three ways of installing cabinet backs are illustrated in figures 104, 105, and 106. While the overlapping back is the easiest to install, it is unsatisfactory in those instances when the layered edge of the back will show, i.e., when veneer is used. The regular inset back is acceptable, but it is difficult to get a perfectly snug fit unless the pieces have been cut and assembled without error. The inset rabbet back is by far the best, providing a snug fit while allowing for a certain margin of error. However, unless you have the power tools to cut the rabbets, it may not be worth your while.

For most backs, 1/4'' veneer is sufficient unless it is going to have to support a lot of weight while hanging unsupported on

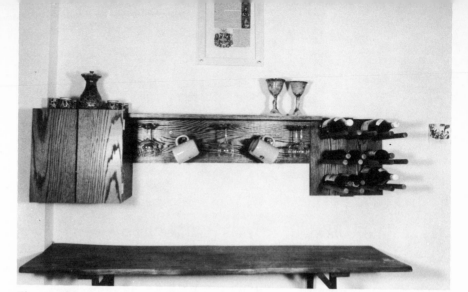

Figure 102

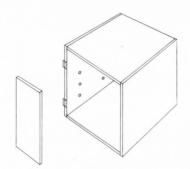

Figure 103

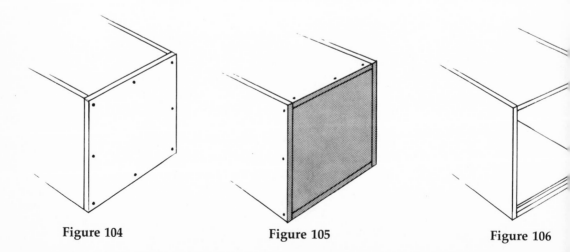

Figure 104   **Figure 105**   **Figure 106**

a wall. While it is certainly preferable to make the back out of the same sort of hardwood veneer as the frame and doors, this is not strictly necessary. A cheaper softwood veneer can be employed, since it normally won't be very much in evidence if it is stained the same color, especially after the cabinet has been filled with the things going into it. Since veneer is usually sold in 4' × 4' or 4' × 8' sheets, buying a large sheet of 1/4" veneer for a small back is not really economically feasible unless you plan to use the remainder at some future date. If you are left with an extra piece of the 3/4" veneer from the frame, you can always use this for the back.

The doors are attached using swaged hinges, either surface-mounted or mortised in (figure 103). Piano hinges running the length of the door are also attractive and are quite easy to cut to the exact length and install. Their use also eliminates the need for mortising to get rid of the space between the door and the cabinet. Two magnetic catches keep the doors in place.

Either standard metal shelf holders or 1" lengths of wooden dowels inserted into the 1/2" deep holes can be used to hold shelves. The edges of the veneer that show on the frame and shelves can be covered with a solid-wood edging.

Simple brass knobs for the doors add a nice touch, although any hardware to your liking can be used.

The center piece of the unit is constructed of two solid planks of wood attached at right angles to each other, fastened with 1-1/4" × 8 wood screws (figure 107). Dowels for hanging stemware are mounted into the wall piece (figure 108) in the same manner as in Project 2 (page 117). If the shelf is going to bear substantial weight, anchor one or both of the edges to the adjacent surfaces: In this case, the front left corner is anchored to the side of the cabinet.

The back of the wine and whiskey rack is formed by gluing together two solid planks or using one sheet of veneer. Several 1" holes are drilled about 2" apart, and 1" dowels are then inserted and glued in the same manner we have already shown (figure 109). The dowels should be long enough to ac-

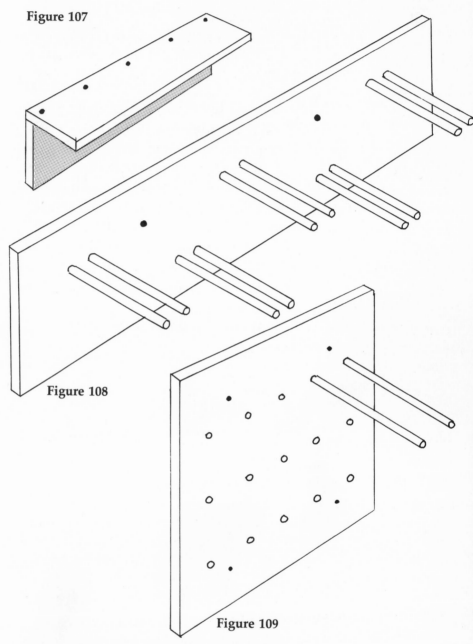

Figure 107

Figure 108

Figure 109

commodate your standard-size bottles—in most cases about 14″. (Your Galiano bottle is best stored somewhere else.)

Stain and finish the unit to your preference (in this case a walnut stain was used) and then mount securely on the wall. Skål!

11 Bookcase and Cabinet

The basic bookcase design is shown in figure 110. As illustrated, it is conceived of as an independent modular unit to which other bookcases or cabinet units can be added and used in various combinations.

The bookcase is normally constructed of 1 × 10 or 1 × 12 solid lumber, either hardwood or softwood. It is joined at the corners using either butt or dado joints and fastened with 1-1/4'' × 8 flathead wood screws that are counterbored and concealed with either wood putty, dowels, or wooden plugs.

If the bookcase is to sit directly on the floor, it can be constructed with a base strip of 1 × 2 or 1 × 3 lumber, which is attached either flush or recessed from the frame front. This strip serves to elevate the bookcase from the floor, moving the objects on the first shelf out of kicking range and giving the bookcase a somewhat more "finished" appearance. If the bookcase is to sit on top of another unit (as in figures 111 and 112), simply eliminate the strip. Or if you want to retain design flexibility, enabling your bookcase to sit on another unit in the future, attach a temporary frame of 2 × 2's or 2 × 3's to the bottom of the bookcase.

The maximum width of the bookcase depends on the lumber you are using, as the most important consideration is to prevent the bowing of the shelves from the weight of what is sitting on them. In the case of softwood like pine, the span should not exceed 2-1/2' to 3', depending on how much the shelves are going to support. In the case of hardwood, a span of 4' (or more) for the shelves should be all right.

This bookcase design utilizes adjustable shelves. They are supported by either 1'' wooden dowels or metal shelf brackets, which fit into a series of 1/4''-diameter holes drilled either 1'' or 2'' apart (vertically) and 1/2'' deep. Use a square and accurate measuring device when marking the places for the

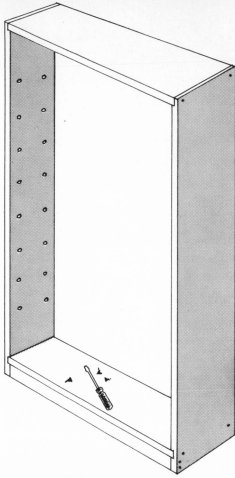

Figure 110

Figure 111

holes to be drilled to insure that the shelves will sit level when the unit is completed.

If you do not anticipate the need for adjustable shelves, the bookcase can be constructed with fixed shelves fitted into dado grooves cut into the bookcase sides and then nailed or screwed into place.

The back of the bookcase can be attached in one of three ways: overlapped, recessed, or rabbeted. See the discussion and illustrations in Project 10 (page 143) for the advantages and disadvantages of each of these.

You may prefer that the bookcase have no back, allowing the wall behind it to show through. This can create an interesting effect, and it certainly gives the bookcase a less bulky appearance and feel, particularly if the wall or wall covering is a light color. If you choose not to have a back, the unit should be firmly attached to the wall in several places to stabilize it. Two corner braces at about the middle of the unit are usually adequate.

Figure 112

Figure 113

A variety of different cabinet designs can be used in combination with the bookcase unit. Two designs are illustrated here (figures 113 and 114, which are details of figures 111 and 112, respectively), and two others are shown in Project 10 (page 143) and Project 13 (page 156).

The frame of the cabinet unit is constructed basically in the same fashion as the bookcase unit just described. The major differences lie in the facts that (1) cabinets are often deeper than bookshelves and thus require the use of either veneer sheets or several solid butted planks for the frame, and (2) cabinets have doors.

Figure 114

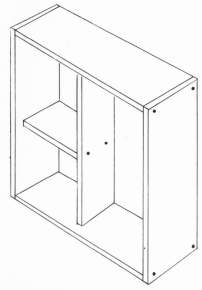

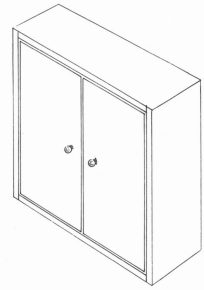

Figure 115   **Figure 116**

Two ways of attaching doors are shown here. Two additional ways are illustrated in the projects mentioned above. In the first design here (figures 115 and 116), the doors are recessed into the frame so that their fronts are flush with the front of the frame. Piano hinges cut to size are the best looking and the easiest way to hang doors such as these, although other types of hinges can be used. Hanging doors like these requires that the frame be square and that the door sizes be accurate, since any sizable errors will prevent the doors from fitting properly. There is very little tolerance for mistakes with this type of door. Getting and keeping the frame square are aided considerably by attaching an accurately cut back, and this should always be done with all cabinets before measuring and cutting the doors.

The second cabinet design (figures 117 and 118) utilizes vertical wood strips attached to the front of the frame and on which the doors are then mounted. Overlapping doors such as these give you a little more tolerance for error (though they shouldn't encourage it!). This design also gives those of you who want absolutely no hinge hardware to show the option of using invisible hinges (Soss hinges) instead of piano hinges for attaching the doors.

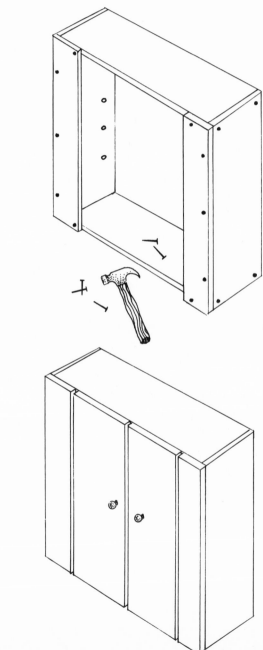

Figure 117

Figure 118

When assembling the doors, first attach them to the strips with whatever hinges you choose before cutting their final width. Then lay the strips and the doors on the frame to get the measurement for proper width. Cut the doors to this width and then attach the strips to the frame.

If the doors are 12'' or less in width, you can use solid lumber for them, avoiding the problem of veneer edges. If the doors are wider than 12'', you must either use veneer or solid pieces attached or glued together. If you use veneer, a nice touch is to cut the two doors from a single sheet of wood, so that you get a matching, continuous grain across both doors.

Once the doors are hung, stain and finish to taste, and then attach knobs and catches.

12 Modular Bookcases

This unique bookcase design (figure 119) is striking as well as highly functional. It is modular in the sense that sections can be added or subtracted with ease. The adjustable shelves and the option to vary the length of shelves permit you to carve out and create the spaces you need. In addition to being simple and inexpensive to construct, the real virtue of the design lies in its originality and openness. Traditional bookshelves by and large have a strictly utilitarian function; they are not made to be noticed. These shelves are as pleasing aesthetically as they are functional. Also, traditional bookshelves normally present a solid, undifferentiated front, a veritable wall of book spines. These shelves present an open, textured appearance, incorporating themselves into the overall design statement of the room, yet standing alone as a highly unique piece of furniture.

The frame standards for these bookcases are best constructed of 1 × 4 stock in hardwood or 2 × 4 in softwood, with butt joints fastened with flathead wood screws (1-1/2'' × 8 or 2-1/2'' × 12, respectively), counterbored and concealed with wood putty, plugs, or dowels. A spacer piece midway between the top and bottom is necessary to prevent bowing (figure 120).

Several 1/4''-deep holes for adjustable shelf brackets are drilled 1'' or 2'' apart on the insides of the standards. This operation should be completed before the standards are put together.

The materials for the units depend entirely on your preference. The unit pictured here utilized solid red oak for the standards, and lauan (Philippine mahogany) for the shelves. Once stained and finished, each standard should be attached to the wall at top and bottom.

Figure 119

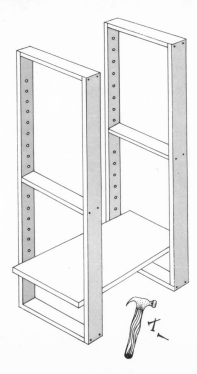

Figure 120

13 Modular Bookcases and Cabinets

This unit (figure 121) utilizes the same bookcase design as in Project 12 (page 154). The cabinets in this unit are designed to fit inside the bookcase standards. Their exact dimensions are thus dependent on the dimensions of the bookcases themselves. As independent modular units, the cabinets can always be added to the bookcases or can be removed and used somewhere else by themselves.

The woods used in the cabinet unit can vary. In this unit, lauan (Philippine mahogany) was used for the frame, shelves, and mitered front border; oak veneer was used for the doors and side strips. If the doors are less than 12″ wide, you can use solid lumber for them and the side strips; if they are more than 12″ wide, you can glue two smaller planks together. Using veneer for the doors is somewhat easier, and it has the advantage of permitting you to cut both doors and side pieces out of the same sheet, giving you a continuous, matching grain across the cabinet fronts.

The basic frame of the cabinet is constructed using simple butt joints and 1-1/4″ × 8 flathead wood screws, counterbored and concealed (figure 122). It is essential that a back be fitted for the cabinet to insure the rigidity and squareness of the unit. The three basic ways of attaching a back are explained in Project 10 (page 143). Before assembly, 1/4″-deep holes should be drilled on the inside of the cabinet sides to accommodate adjustable shelf holders.

Once the frame and back are assembled, this design calls for a mitered 1 × 3 border to be attached to the front of the cabinet frame with 1-1/4″ × 8 flathead wood screws, counterbored and concealed (figure 123). This border has the functional purpose of permitting the cabinet frame to sit between the bookcase standards without interfering with the swing of the doors. The adjustable shelves used inside the cabinet should

Figure 121

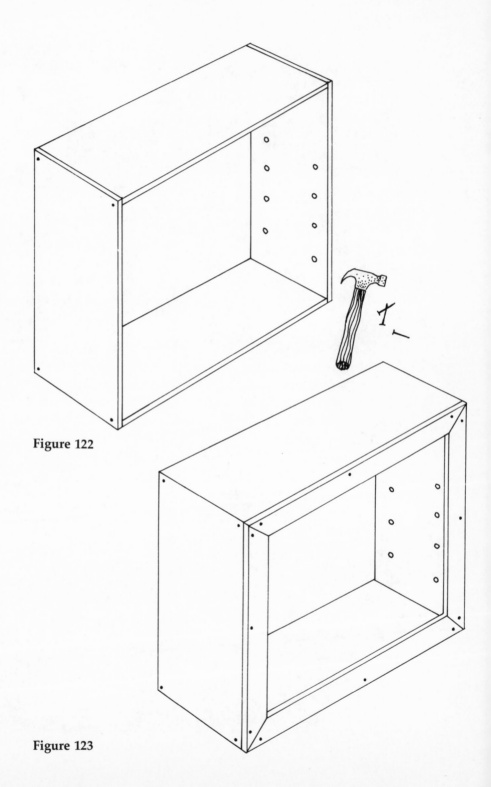

Figure 122

Figure 123

already be there when the border is attached, since they may not fit through the completed opening.

After the border is in place, cut the doors and the side strips to the appropriate sizes (figure 124). Since they both overlap the border, exact tolerances are not essential, provided that both doors are mounted the same height. As mentioned, if veneer is used, the doors and side pieces should be cut out of a single piece of wood to present a matching, continuous grain. After cutting to appropriate size, attach each door to a side strip, using either "continuous" piano hinges or Soss invisible hinges. Then lay the two doors and side strips out on the border in their correct positions. Attach the side strips to the border with 1-1/4" × 8 flathead wood screws, counterbored and concealed. You may find it helpful to keep a piece of cardboard between the two doors when attaching the side strips in order to keep a proper tolerance between them.

Attach whatever knobs (if any) and catches you desire, and then strain and finish. If you are mixing woods and stains, as in this piece here, it is actually better to stain the pieces before assembly and then apply the finish once assembly has been completed.

Figure 124

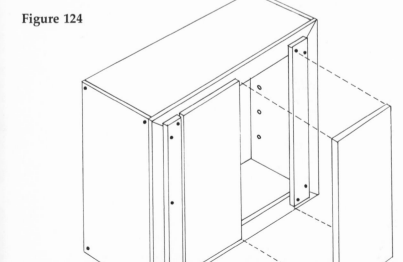

14 Wall Unit I

This particular wall unit (figure 125) is comprised of three individual, completely independent sections. There are several advantages to such a design. First, it is easier to construct than if it were one piece, and it is also a much stronger unit once it is constructed. Second, it permits you to arrange the three units in different combinations in the room. Third, it allows you to use each of the units by itself or with one of the other two in case you move to a different space with different requirements or in case your needs change in the space that you are already occupying. Our feeling is that any unit 6' or larger should be divided up into 3' or 4' independent sections in order to enjoy these benefits.

This particular unit is comprised of certain fixed-shelf sections (the desk and the audio-visual sections) as well as certain sections with adjustable shelves. The wood for the frame of the unit is 5/4'' #2 pine (1-1/8'' thick), while the shelves are stan-

Figure 125

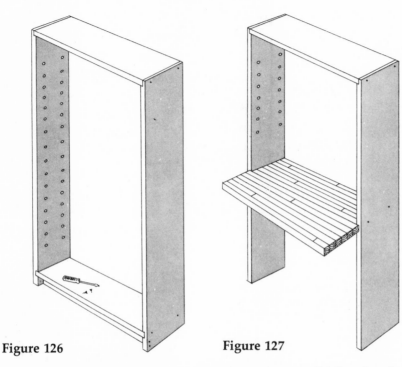

Figure 126   **Figure 127**

dard 1'' #2 pine. It is often quite nice to use thicker lumber for the frame of a large unit: It has a more substantial look to it, it solves certain support problems (especially when adjustable shelves are used), and the eye tends to notice it more, since virtually all the lumber we are exposed to is of the 1'' variety. Hardwood in this thickness is prohibitive in price, but 5/4'' pine and 2'' construction fir and spruce (Project 15, page 164) are both monetarily manageable.

The first section of the unit is a simple bookcase section, framed with 5/4'' pine as mentioned and joined with dado joints and 2'' × 10 flathead wood screws, counterbored and concealed (figure 126). A series of 1/4''-deep holes are drilled before assembly for the shelf supports—either metal or 1'' long × 1/4'' diameter wooden dowels. With thick lumber such as this, a back is really optional, and if your floor is level, the bookcase may not even have to be attached to the wall. The baseboard on the bottom of the illustrated piece is recessed, though it could just as easily be mounted flush with the front edge of the unit.

The second unit is like the first except that it has a 2'' butcher-block desk top set into 2'' dado grooves cut into the sides of the unit (figure 127). The support of these grooves is more than adequate to support the butcherblock. Tops other than butcherblock can also be mounted in the same fashion. Since the unit is imbalanced by the desk top, it does have to be attached to either the wall or the adjacent units (after staining and finishing). In this case, it was attached to the adjacent units with wood screws.

The third section (figure 128) is a little more complicated than the first two for two reasons. First, it has a fixed arrangement of horizontal and vertical pieces that form compartments for

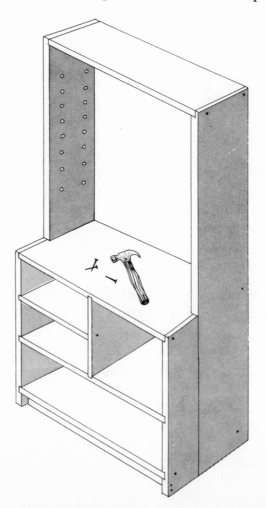

Figure 128

the audio-visual equipment. Second, since such equipment is deeper than the standard shelf width of the rest of the units (either 10″ or 12″), this section has to be made deeper than the rest of the unit. This is done by gluing an additional piece of wood the appropriate width and height to each of the vertical frame members. After the glue dries, the joint where they meet is sanded level and smooth. The appropriate dadoes are cut into it, and the unit is then assembled using wood screws. The top and bottom 5/4″ shelves for this unit are glued together in the same manner as the sides. The 1″ shelves between them are normally available in already laminated sizes (1 × 16, 1 × 18, 1 × 24), which you can trim to the exact size you need (or you can glue these up yourself).

When figuring out a design for equipment such as this, remember to allow a few inches for the equipment to "breathe" so that it won't overheat. Experiment with the spaces you need until you arrive at a design which is both functional and balanced in appearance.

This particular unit was stained a walnut and finished with two coats of satin-finish polyurethane, but naturally you can stain and finish it in any way you prefer.

After the units are stained and finished, you can attach them to each other using 1-3/4″ × 8 wood screws, using clamps to hold the pieces together until the screws are drawn tight. You could do this before you stain and finish, but this means that the interior sides will not be completely finished in case they are ever used as separate units.

15 Wall Unit II

The wall unit pictured in figure 129 is similar in overall conceptual design to the unit we just considered in Project 14 (page 160), though it differs in several important respects. The major difference is that this is a completely fixed-shelf design. While the unit in Project 14 has two fixed-shelf sections (desk, audiovisual section), the bulk of its space is adjustable. Though the fixed-shelf design has the obvious disadvantage of relative inflexibility once completed, it has two significant advantages also, First, the shelves can all be dadoed into the sides, making the unit extremely strong, or they can be attached with wood screws, thus permitting them to be moved at some future date. Either method performs the service of preventing the shelves from warping. This is particularly important when using softwood such as pine (even more important with 2" construction-grade spruce or fir, which was used in this project). This type of lumber, while reasonable in price, is seldom completely dry, and it will shrink, warp, and split excessively if it is not firmly jointed or attached with wood screws.

A second advantage to the fixed-shelf design is that it enables you to create spaces within the unit by inserting vertical pieces (of course, this is possible with adjustable shelves, but it cannot be accomplished as easily or as well). The use of verticals thus enables you to frame, outline, and highlight special or unusual objects while breaking up the monotony of simple horizontal shelves. It gives the appearance of a custom-made piece of furniture (which it is) by giving these objects a "built-in" look. The overall mosaic of such a unit can really be quite striking.

Though the construction details are relatively simple for a unit like this, the planning and preparation are not. First, an exhaustive inventory of the things that the unit is to house is required, and to some extent, your needs for the future should be anticipated. Second, working out a design that is functional and balanced, with an overall pleasing appearance, is re-

Figure 129

quired. It may take some time to work it out exactly as you want it on paper, but it will be time very well spent.

The wood used here was 2 × 10 construction-grade fir, but 5/4'' pine or any other wood will work just as well. Dadoes should be about 1/2'' deep for 2'' lumber and 1/4'' deep for 1'' lumber. Use counterbored or countersunk 2'' × 10 flathead wood screws for the 2'' lumber, 1-1/4'' × 8 for the 1'' lumber. Vertical pieces need not be dadoed in; they are simply screwed. This will give you some flexibility for modifying the design by moving, adding, or subtracting vertical pieces.

The piece diagramed in figure 130 represents the end component in the photograph. The entire unit was comprised of four separate, independent components such as this one, which were joined together with wood screws.

One possibility for combining the advantages of adjustable- and fixed-shelf units is to combine these features, making certain specialized spaces fixed-shelf sections of the unit and making other sections adjustable for ordinary bookshelf use.

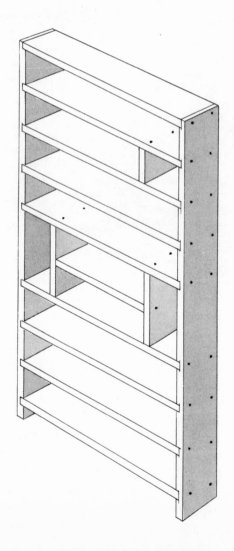

Figure 130

16 Coffee Table

The unusual lines of this table (figure 131) make it a visually captivating structure as well as a highly functional piece of furniture. As with the other tables, it can be made in virtually any size lumber and in a variety of different woods. This particular table was made using 4 × 4 maple for the legs, and 1 × 5 oak for the sides. A 3/8''-thick piece of glass was used for the top. Because of the span, hardwood is best for the sides, although softwood would be acceptable. Legs can be made of maple or oak, both of which are very attractive, or another hardwood of your choosing that you can find in the 4 × 4 size. Cedar, a softwood, is readily available at most lumberyards and has an attractive grain and aroma. If you are working primarily with hand tools, using a softwood like cedar may be necessary, since channeling out the groove in hardwood 4 × 4's really requires power assistance unless you are prepared to spend considerable time and effort.

The heart of the construction design is the channeled legs (figure 132). The channeling removes much of the feeling of bulk from the 4 × 4's, giving the table a surprisingly light appearance considering its size and the durability of its construction. The channeling also provides the means for joining the table together in a way that is extremely strong yet with no visible fastening on external surfaces.

Cutting the channel can be done in a number of ways. By hand, the tool best employed is a backsaw to cut the sides of the groove perpendicular to each other until they join. The channel can also be routed out using a straight-cut router bit. Don't try to take out too much of the channel at once with the router, particularly with hardwood. Remove the wood gradually, using an adjustable guide (or board clamped as a guide) until you attain the proper depth and width.

Using a radial-arm or a table saw, you can either use the saw blade set to the proper depth to rip the two sides of the groove

167

Figure 131

or you can use a dado attachment (in a rip position) to create the channel.

After the channel has been cut out, you may find that some sanding is in order, since it is difficult to make a perfect cut. Use a belt sander for quick removal of stock and a finishing sander (or sand by hand) to finish up.

Next construct the sides of the table as a simple box frame, using butt joints and countersunk 1-1/4″ × 8 flathead screws (figure 133). There is no need to conceal these fasteners, since they will not be visible once the legs are attached.

Finally, attach the frame to the legs, either by gluing or by counterboring 2″ × 10 flathead wood screws from the inside of the frame into the legs (figure 134). Clamps are extremely useful in holding the legs in place while you are doing this. Fill the counterbored holes with dowels, plugs, or putty. The distance from the top of the frame to the tops of the legs should be the same dimension as the thickness of the tabletop you're using so that the top will be flush with the tops of the legs. If possi-

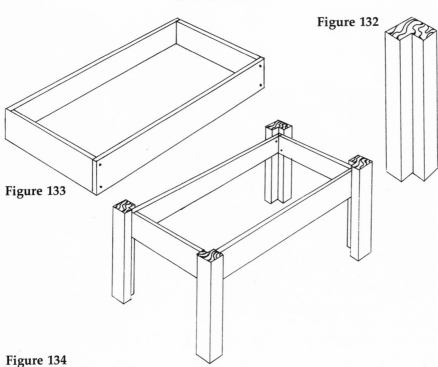

Figure 132

Figure 133

Figure 134

ble, take the measurement for the length and width of the tabletop *after* the table has been constructed. If you already have
the top, the outside dimensions of the assembled frame should
be slightly larger than the dimensions of the tabletop in order
to insure a proper fit (clearance of 1/16'' to 1/8'' in length and
width).

We think glass is the most effective tabletop, though a piece of
wood could be used instead. The glass, either smoked or clear,
gives the entire table a transparency that reduces its look of
bulk and enables you to see the entire structure of the table.
The glass can be obtained from your local glazier, and though
a 1/4'' thickness should be more than sufficient for strength,
3/8'' has an exceptionally nice appearance, particularly on the
larger-size tables.

The table in the photograph was left natural (unstained) and
then finished with two coats of polyurethane. However, your
table can be stained whatever color you prefer (experiment
first!), and you can even contrast the colors of the legs and
sides with light and dark colors.

17 Desk I

This desk (figure 135, viewed from the back), which can also be used to display items, is really an extension of the design for the coffee table illustrated in Project 16 (page 167). As such, it has the same advantages of design and construction that the table has, with the added feature of considerable storage/display space that is visible and accessible and that can also be locked.

The frame for the unit should be constructed of 1 × 6 or 1 × 8 hardwood (oak here), depending on its overall dimensions and the use that it will be put to. The front and two sides should have a dado groove running their lengths (figure 136), into which the bottom of the desk will fit. The two smaller pieces in back adjacent to the fold-down door should not have a dado groove, since the door should be flush with these pieces when in the closed position. (If possible, cut the door and the two adjacent pieces from the same board so that the grain of the wood will match up and be continuous all the way across.) Attach all sides of the frame with butt joints and 1-1/4″ × 8 flathead wood screws, counterbored and concealed (figure 137). The dado grooves on three sides will be more than adequate support for the desk bottom, provided it is made of 3/4″ veneer. (The veneer for the bottom should match the frame unless you intend to cover it for display purposes.)

The legs for the desk are identical to the legs for the coffee table in Project 16 (page 167), only longer. They are constructed in the same manner described in that project. Once the legs are cut and channeled, attach them to the frame, using 2″ × 10 flathead, counterbored and concealed, wood screws from inside the frame (figure 138). Use clamps when assembling.

As with the coffee table, recess the frame from the tops of the legs the same distance as the thickness of the top you are using. In the case of glass, this should be 1/4″ or 3/8″.

Figure 135

Figure 136

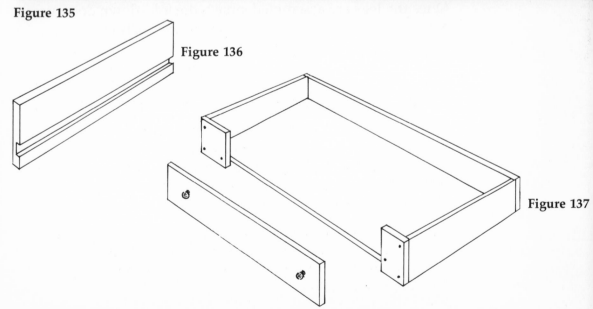

Figure 137

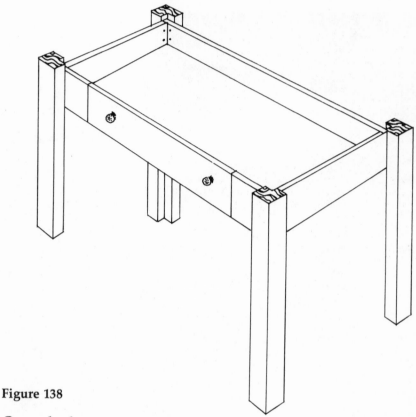

Figure 138

Once the legs are assembled, attach the fold-down door, using a piano hinge running its length (they are easily cut to size). In order to do this, you will have to attach a piece of 1 × 1 along the lower edge of the desk bottom to make it flush with the bottom of the frame and allow the proper installation of the hinge. Allow 1/16'' to 1/8'' clearance on each edge of the door.

Next install one or two catches to hold the door in place when closed; either a strong magnet or a positive roller catch is good. Attach two knobs—brass, porcelain, or something comparable. Finally, install a lock at one end if you want to keep out prying fingers.

Stain and finish to taste, and drop in the glass for the top. Remember, measure and order the glass for the top *after* the unit is assembled, if possible, leaving a clearance of 1/16'' to 1/8'' in each direction.

18 Desk II/Dresser

The desk design is comprised of two units—the desk table and the drawers (figure 139). They can be used together or independently. Additional units can be added to form a long, continuous work (or play) surface.

The two units were constructed using 2'' clear pine for the frames and 1-1/2'' butcherblock for the tops, though other types of wood are equally workable. The desk unit is a simple construction of two side pieces and a 2 × 4 (or 4 × 4) stretcher attached to them by counterbored and concealed 2-1/2'' × 12 flathead wood screws (figure 140). The overlapping top is then attached to the tops of the sides, using 2'' corner braces.

When making drawers, always make the frame into which they fit first and the drawers second, to enable you to get close tolerances on the fit, and also to avoid the possibility of the drawer's being too large for the frame.

The frame of the drawer unit is made in the same fashion as a bookcase with fixed, dadoed shelves, held together using 2-1/2'' × 10 flathead wood screws and/or glue (figure 141). A back should also be attached to the unit (see Project 10, page 143). The top is then attached to the top of the unit with 2'' × 10 flathead wood screws from underneath.

The drawers themselves are usually made from solid pine or veneer. The clearance for the drawer should be about 1/8'' to 3/16'' vertically and horizontally, and each of the frame openings should be measured separately, since they sometimes vary in size. The sides of each drawer have a dado groove cut 1/4'' to 1/2'' from one edge to accommodate the bottom of the drawer (figure 142)—usually 1/4'' inch thick for small drawers, 3/8'' for larger. When taking measurements, give the bottom 1/16'' to 1/8'' clearance in each direction inside the groove. The groove should be approximately 1/4'' to 3/8'' deep. If you are using a router, radial-arm saw, or table saw to cut the groove, you will find it somewhat easier to cut it on

173

Figure 139

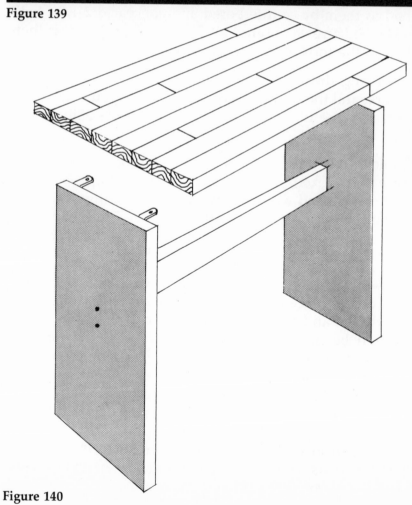

Figure 140

Figure 141

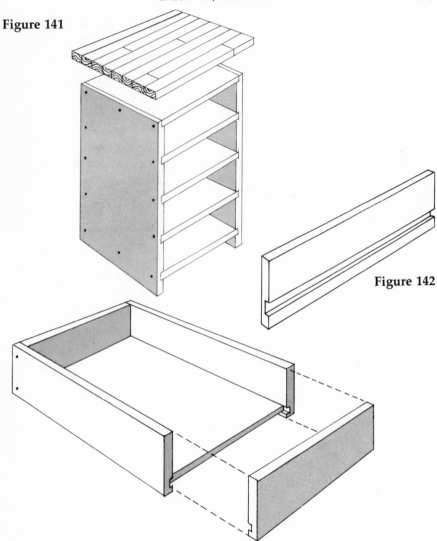

Figure 142

Figure 143

longer boards and then cut these up to the individual drawer sides. Be very careful in measuring and cutting the pieces for the drawers, as it is quite easy to make mistakes. Once they are cut, assemble three sides around the drawer bottom with 6d or 8d finishing nails (or 1-1/4″ × 8 flathead wood screws, countersunk), and then attach the fourth side (figure 143). The two sides of the drawer should overlap the front and back for added strength.

After the drawer frame and bottom have been assembled, attach the drawer front to the drawer frame with 1-1/4'' × 8 flathead wood screws, countersunk, from the inside of the drawer
(figure 144). The drawer front should overlap the drawer
frame around it by 1/4'' if the frame is 1'' wood, 1/2'' if the
frame is 5/4'' or 2''. Attach the knobs or pulls to the drawer
and slide it into position.

Overlapping drawers are superior to flush-mounted drawers
in that they allow you some margin for error, and they also
have a cleaner appearance once they are completed.

This same basic design for the desk-drawer unit can be used
for any size dresser (figure 145). Instead of complete shelves
between the drawers, however, you can use solid-lumber bars
in front only, with either wooden cleats screwed to the inside
sides of the dresser (figure 146) or metal drawer slides and Tef-
lon wheels attached to the inside sides of the dresser and sides
of the drawer (figure 147).

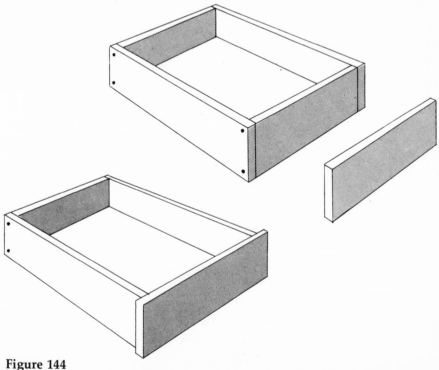

Figure 144

Figure 145

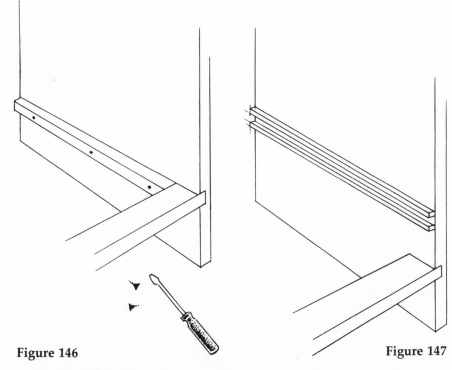

Figure 146   **Figure 147**

19 Tea Cart

This cart (figure 148) functions basically as a serving cart, but is also an attractive and useful piece in a stationary position. The shelves of the cart illustrated here are made of 1-1/2'' maple butcherblock. The frame of the cart is 2 × 2 solid birch, though any hardwood of this approximate size is appropriate. The frame members are notched with dado grooves (figure 149) and then attached to the shelves with 2'' × 10 flathead wood screws, which are counterbored and concealed with either wood putty, dowels, or wooden plugs. Instead of using screws, you can glue the joints if you prefer. (Use clamps while glue dries.)

Figure 148

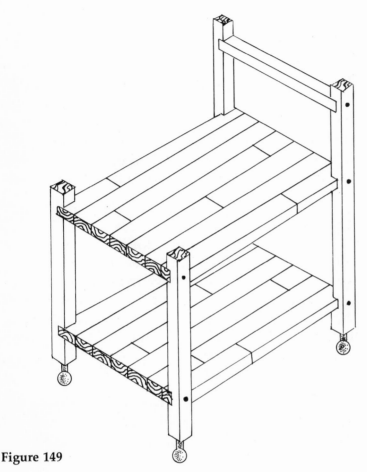

Figure 149

Holes are drilled into the bottoms of the front legs to accommodate casters, and into the rear legs if casters are to be used
there. If wheels are to be used on the rear, attach the axle to the
underside of the lower shelf right in front of the rear legs. The
wheels are then placed on the axle. This set of axle and wheels
was purchased from a local specialty house. You may have to
hunt for them in your area, or you can secure them from a specialty house with a mail-order business. Casters are available
at most hardware stores.

Stain and finish the frame to your liking. The butcherblock can
be kept in good condition with a periodic application of linseed oil and turpentine, or any other oil or varnish finish you
care to apply.

20 Room Divider

This room divider is a very effective piece of furniture for delineating two spaces without completely separating them. The two sides of the unit can reflect the differences in the two rooms—in this case, rustic barnboard planks for the living-room side (figure 150), and natural-finished pine for the kitchen side (figure 151). The unit also has considerable functional use as both a counter and storage space.

The basic frame is constructed of either 1'', 5/4'', or 2'' lumber. Again the problem of unit width is a factor in this decision: If the unit is to be wider than 11-1/2'', then either veneer has to be used or two or more solid planks have to be glued together to form the wider piece. In this case, prelaminated #2 pine planks in a 1 × 18 size were used. These are often available at your local lumberyard, as well as 1 × 16 and 1 × 24 sizes. If you prefer other kinds of solid wood, you'll probably have to do the gluing (and sanding) yourself.

The basic frame of the unit is constructed along the same lines as one of the components of Project 15 (page 164), using dado joints and flathead wood screws (figure 152), counterbored and concealed. As noted, one side of the unit here is faced with rustic barnboard. This gives the unit rigidity and insures its squareness, particularly important for the sliding doors on the other side. Of course, any kind of planking, or a single sheet of veneer, can be used for this purpose.

The counter top is formed by setting a 1-1/2'' slab of butcher-block on the top shelf and attaching it with wood screws from underneath.

Once the unit is assembled, the sliding doors are cut and installed, using the same wood for the doors as for the frame (preferably). The grooves that the doors slide in are formed by screwing 1 × 1 clear pine strips to the top and bottom of each opening with 1-1/4'' × 8 flathead wood screws, counterbored and concealed (figure 153). The tracks should be set 1/16'' farther apart than the widths of the doors to allow for easy slid-

Figure 150

Figure 151

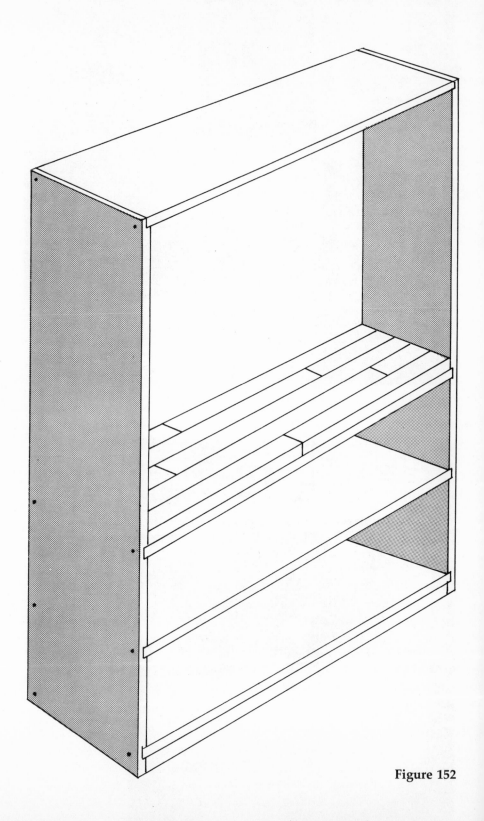

Figure 152

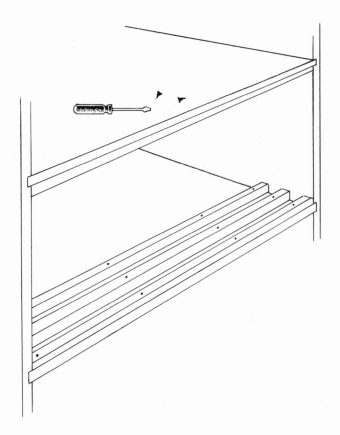

Figure 153

ing. The doors are each cut to a size of one-half the total length of the shelf plus 1-1/2'', thus giving you a door overlap of 3''. They are installed as the tracks are put into place. Manufactured plastic or metal tracks can be used if you so desire.

Knobs for the doors either should be less than 3/4'' deep or should be placed near the ends of the doors so that you get a full slide from the rear door without the knob catching on the front door.

If possible, the doors and insides of the cabinets should be stained and finished before the doors are installed. The rest of the unit can be stained and finished after it is completed.

21 Trestle Table

The design of this trestle table (figure 154) is literally centuries old. However, despite its antiquity, its clean, simple lines make it completely appropriate for modern usage and in combination with those modern-furniture designs that also exhibit clean, simple lines.

The table can be made in virtually any size, although 4' to 8' in length is the optimal range. The thickness of the wood can also vary, although it is best made with wood 1'' to 2'' thick. Naturally, using a hardwood, such as cherry (pictured here), oak, or walnut, is ideal, but that can be fairly expensive. Pine is considerably cheaper and is also more readily available in the thicker boards. The differences between the two (i.e., pine and fine hardwood) lie in the natural beauty of the wood and the durability. Hardwood, particularly boards as thick as this, are also more difficult to work with, especially without power tools. The wood that you use is thus really dependent on your own unique situation, though sometime after it is made you don't want to say, "I wish I had spent the extra money and used a better-quality wood" (a not uncommon occurrence). After all, a table like this is built to last a lifetime.

The top is the most important part of the table, since it is the part that is most visible and receives the most use. Though there was a time when planks were available as wide as a tabletop, such is not the case now; the top must be constructed by gluing individual boards together. This technique actually makes the top more resistant to warpage than a single piece would be.

The individual planks should be 6'' to 8'' wide, though different widths are acceptable. If possible, the boards should be surfaced square on all four sides when you receive them; if they're not, and you don't have a power jointer or planer, it is worth paying someone a moderate amount to do it. Trying to square up large boards such as these with hand tools, or even hand power tools, is a very difficult proposition indeed.

Figure 154

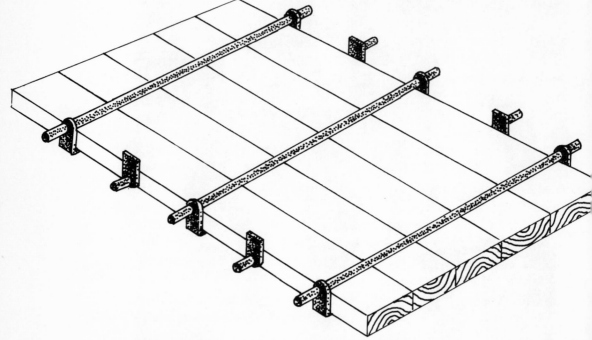

Figure 155A

Once the boards are planed smooth and square, the boards for the top should be cut to the desired length. Any small differences can be sanded smooth after the top is assembled. If you are using a softwood, and you have access to a circular saw, you can cut the boards to a rough length, assemble them, and then finish-cut them after they are glued together, insuring a smooth edge. If you are careful in your cutting, either way should be acceptable.

After this has been completed, lay out the boards in the order you will want them in the top, concealing defects on edges and matching the grain patterns as well as possible. Additionally, as you look at the ends of the boards once in place, the growth rings on successive boards should run in opposite directions (figure 155A). This will help reduce warpage. Mark the boards on the edges so that the order can be reconstructed quickly.

Gluing is the next step. Use a good-quality "yellow" wood glue (e.g., Titebond) and slightly roughen up the edges to be glued with a file to give better adhesion. Lay out the boards to be glued (two sawhorses or the equivalent are handy for assembly of the top). Apply glue liberally to all edges to be glued. Move the boards together into proper alignment. Take a heavy-duty bar or pipe clamp and place it across the center of the table. Use wooden blocks to protect the edges of the table, and tighten the clamp only *moderately* (not completely). Place the next clamp 12″ to 18″ away from this clamp and run it *underneath* the tabletop, and again tighten moderately (figure 155A). The third clamp should be placed underneath the tabletop 12″ to 18″ from the first in the opposite direction from the second. Alternating the position of the clamps like this—alternate sides of the tabletop, alternate directions from the center—prevents the clamps from buckling the top. Continue placing the clamps in this manner until you reach the ends of the table. As you place the clamps on, check continuously the alignment of the boards to insure that they remain even on the top and ends. Once the bar or pipe clamps have been applied with moderate tension, use a C-clamp to clamp each corner of the table to the sawhorses or table it is resting on. This will prevent buckling as you further tighten the bar clamps. Once this is accomplished, gradually tighten the bar clamps, taking turns so that they are tightened as evenly as possible. Allow the glue to dry thoroughly (24 to 48 hours) and remove the clamps. (Gluing a top requires quite a few clamps, and instead of buying them all, you might try borrowing some for this one project.)

The top must now be sanded as level as possible, removing all traces of glue. A belt sander is most appropriate for this rough sanding. Keep it moving in large sweeps to prevent uneven removal of wood, and gradually reduce the grit coarseness of the sandpaper. Once level, complete the sanding with a finishing sander.

The base of the table should be made of the same type and thickness of wood as the top. Start by cutting out the two legs in a shape similar to the photograph and diagrams. Allow an extra 2″ at each end of the pieces for joining into the feet and

Figure 155B

tabletop supports with mortise and tenon joints. Use a band saw or saber saw to cut the sides of the pieces.

The feet of the table are made of 4 × 4's. These should also be of the same or comparable wood as the top. Cut them out in a pattern similar to that shown in figure 155B. This particular pattern is also illustrated in a graph form in figure 156A. A band saw is by far the best tool for this, and if you don't have one, you might see if you can use someone else's for a few minutes to cut the feet (and legs). Otherwise you'll have to use a saber saw with a long blade or cut from both sides.

Once the feet are cut, take each leg and center it on top of one of the feet, outlining its base in pencil. Using a drill with a bit the same diameter as the thickness of the leg, drill a series of consecutive 2''-deep holes within the confines of the outlines. Using a wood chisel, square off the opening to the exact size of the outline. The legs should fit into these mortise holes snugly.

Glue into place, clamping tightly. Once dry, drill two 1/2'' holes through the inside sides of each foot, through the por-

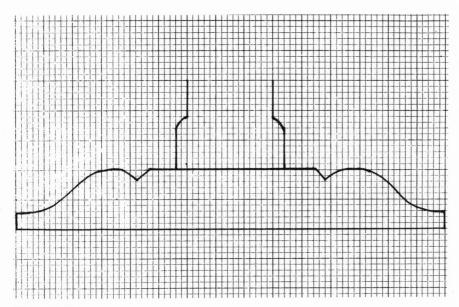

Figure 156A

tion of the leg glued into the foot, and stopping just short of exiting on the other side of the foot. Glue two 1/2″ dowels into the holes, thus locking the mortise-and-tenon joint firmly into place (figure 156B).

Cut the tabletop support members in a pattern similar to that illustrated. (Beveling the ends will make them less visible.) Attach these members to the legs in the same manner as described above for the feet.

The final piece of the pedestal is the stretcher. Its length is the distance between the two legs, plus 10″ for the two tenons. After cutting to the right length, cut the tenons on the ends to the approximate dimensions shown in figure 157. This is best done with a router, or dado attachments to your saw, but it can also be done using hand tools. After it is completed, cut the mortises in the legs for the tenons in the same manner as described previously. On each end, fit the tenon through the mortise tightly, mark the point where it exits on the other side of the leg, and remove the tenon. Drill a hole 1″ in diameter on a tangent with this line. Reinsert the tenon and tap a 1″ dowel 3″ long through the hole to lock the joint. The pedestal should now be completely assembled.

Figure 156B

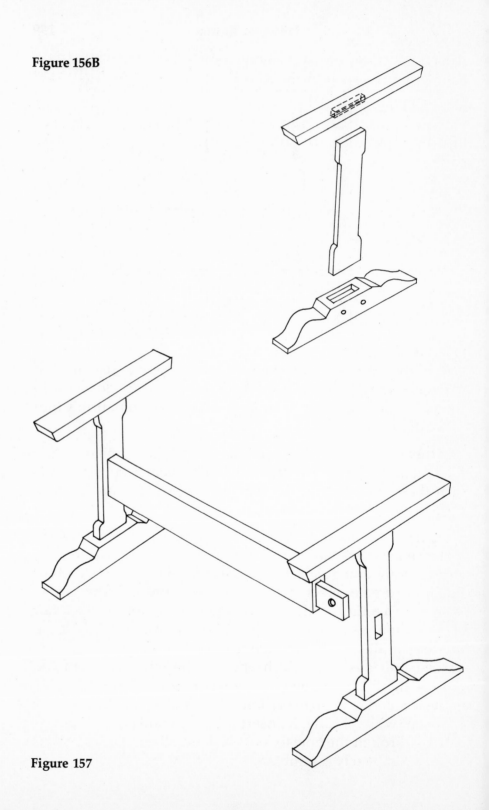

Figure 157

Attach the table supports to the underside of the table, using countersunk wood screws, four for each member.

Stain and finish the table to your preference. Remember to put the same number of finish coats on the bottom as on the top, insuring equal moisture absorption and thus preventing warpage.

A good, hard paste wax will protect the finish of the table from the abuse that it is bound to receive in ordinary usage.